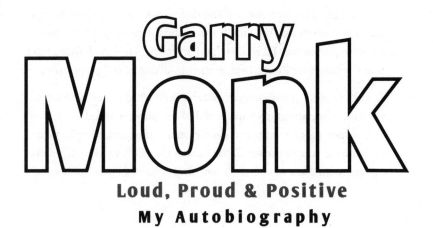

Garry Monk

Loud, Proud & Positive

My Autobiography

with Peter Read

y Lolfa

I'd like to thank Peter Read for all his help and time in writing this book. Thank you to Y Lolfa for giving me the opportunity to tell my story. I'd like to thank my mum and dad who have been there for me through everything. Also, my brother and all my family who have always supported me. I'd like to thank my two girls – my fiancée Lexy and my daughter Remy. Both are my motivation and inspiration.

Thanks to all of my managers, coaches and team mates who have helped me throughout my career, and to the physios and doctors who have helped patch me up and get me out on the field. Thanks to all the fantastic support from all the fans at the clubs I have played at, especially the Jack Army who I will always have a close bond with.

First impression: 2012
© Copyright Garry Monk and Y Lolfa Cyf., 2012

The contents of this book are subject to copyright, and may not be reproduced by any means, mechanical or electronic, without the prior, written consent of the publishers.

The publishers wish to acknowledge the support of
Cyngor Llyfrau Cymru

Cover design: Y Lolfa
Cover photograph: Huw Evans Agency

Thanks to Swansea City FC and
Dimitris Legakis, Athena Photography for the photographs

ISBN: 978 184771 423 7

FSC

Published and printed in Wales
on paper from well maintained forests by
Y Lolfa Cyf., Talybont, Ceredigion SY24 5HE
website www.ylolfa.com
e-mail ylolfa@ylolfa.com
tel 01970 832 304
fax 832 782

Foreword

by Brendan Rodgers

On Tuesday, 24 August 2010 we played one of my first games in charge of Swansea City FC versus Tranmere Rovers at Prenton Park in the Carling Cup. At half-time we were 1–0 down and as I was preparing notes to deliver my speech in the dressing room, a hand went up to apologize to me and the team for the mistake which led to the Tranmere goal. That hand belonged to my skipper, Garry Monk. I recognized instantly the defining moment that had just occurred and, importantly, the conduct I felt which would give us as a group the opportunity to succeed in the future. Garry's action was not normal in this modern day, where players lack the honesty of years gone by, but a refreshing act of loyalty to a group and manager which has continued throughout every single day of my time at Swansea City.

When I arrived at Swansea City in July 2010 I asked the chairman to arrange a meeting with the club captain and myself. After my press commitments on the first day I needed to ensure that Garry knew the importance of his role to the team and to the manager. Whilst talking to him in the main stand at the Liberty

Stadium, I sensed an unswerving commitment in his support of my vision to take the club forward, and his passion for the club which he clearly loves. My perception from watching Garry as a footballer over the years was as a steady, reliable centre-half who was working his way through the leagues. The reality is much more than that. This is a man who is the ultimate professional, who prepares his time every single day to get the most out of his body. His focus and drive to maximize his capability to be the very best he can possibly be is an inspiration to his team mates. His ability on the field and arrival in the Barclays Premier League as a player is a fantastic achievement, but you could also deem it a failure of the coaching system in Britain, because Garry's qualities should have taken him there much earlier in his career.

I have had too many outstanding moments on the field from Garry to mention, but two in particular are clear in my mind. The first was, of course, his game-saving block in the epic play-off final versus Reading. Having been 3–0 up and Reading then clawing their way back to 3–2, a goal-bound shot by Noel Hunt, the Reading striker, looked to be heading straight into the middle of the net when Garry made an incredible game-saving challenge that prevented the equalizer. What was also remarkable about his performance at Wembley was the pain and numbness in his right foot – not many players would have played for fear of being exposed in a game better known as the "£90 million game". To perform to the level he did showed tremendous courage and everyone connected with Swansea City that day is indebted to his heroic performance. The second outstanding moment was at Anfield against Liverpool, and a piece of skill that many may not associate with Garry! In one of our passing movements he was closed down and put under pressure by the excellent Liverpool striker, Luis Suárez, but his composure and technique to clip the ball over his head to a team mate left the striker stunned, and for me demonstrated a side of his game that has been underrated.

Garry's story has taken him from the parks of Torquay to the pinnacle of Wembley, a real magic carpet ride through every level of the British game, and a story which will provide inspiration and hope for many youth and senior players in the years to come.

Brendan Rodgers
Swansea City FC Team Manager

Chapter One

I WAS BROUGHT up in a football-mad family. My father, Alan, was a keen footballer in and around the local London leagues. His cousin is Ian Gillard who played in the First Division for Queens Park Rangers, while his brother Raymond was offered the chance to play for Tottenham Hotspur in the early 1960s which he declined, and my cousin, Warren Monk, was on the books of QPR as an apprentice.

Although I was born in Bedford, I grew up in Torquay where the family moved to when I was just four years old. From an early age I was also football mad. I'd go to school but my mind wasn't always on the work in hand. Most of the reports said, 'If Garry puts his mind to this subject then he could achieve something in life.' The trouble was that during lessons all I wanted to do was be outside playing sport, especially football.

My mum and dad decided to take me along to the local Cubs pack. I enrolled, but I didn't last long. They threw me out, or should I say, asked my mum not to bring me back. They said I was a disruptive influence on the other boys, as all the time I was encouraging them to come outside and play sport with me. I thought they should learn more about football rather than how to tie knots! When I eventually left school, I didn't come out with particularly good grades. I suppose, looking back now, I should have knuckled down and worked harder. Knowing what I know now, I realize that to make it as a footballer you need a lot of luck, as well as talent and skill.

When I was in secondary school I signed for a local boys team, Torquay Colts FC. My brother Stuart, who is a year and a half older than me, was a good player and he played for teams in Devon as well. Growing up, people always thought that he was the more talented of the two of us, and had more potential to go on into professional football. But Stuart was the kind of player who wanted someone else to score, rather than himself. He had the skill, I had aggression to go with the skill.

When I started playing I was always a centre forward rather than a defender. It wasn't until I was twelve that I switched to defence. As a youngster I found myself playing against boys who were at least two years older than me. I was so competitive and determined that, if anyone got the ball off me, even though many of them were bigger and stronger than me, I would chase them the length of the pitch until I got it back.

I represented Devon at schoolboy county level. Playing for them, surrounded by good players, I began to believe I might actually have a chance of doing something in football. We reached the quarter-finals of the English Schools' Trophy, before losing to Sussex. As well as playing whenever I could, I immersed myself in the game and watched as much football as I could. Italian football was a massive influence on me at that time, and I watched it on television every Sunday afternoon. AC Milan was the team I liked to see and their star-studded teams, with the likes of Paulo Maldini, Marco Van Basten, George Weah all fantastic players, but my favourite was captain and defender Franco Baresi. He was an unbelievable defender and was great to watch.

Two British players I admired in my youth were Paul Gascoigne and Tony Adams. Although Gazza had troubles later in his life, I loved his personality and skills and watching him throw himself into every game. Because my brother supported Arsenal and I loved Gazza, I just had to support Spurs. Despite that fact, I still found myself drawn to Tony Adams, although he played for Arsenal. As a player, he had everything. Even during the period of alcoholism, his attitude was so good that, I was told, he once woke up on a park bench, realized he was playing that evening, turned up at Highbury and was man of the match.

I think I was attracted by Adams' leadership skills. From an early age of playing, I think I've always been a leader. As I've grown and developed as a player, I've realized how to affect and influence the people around me. After becoming more comfortable with my position, I've got better at communicating with other players. Part of the excitement of football for me is having other players around me, and being able to influence them. I really enjoy being involved in the tactical battle against the opposition.

While I was playing for Torquay Colts FC

under-13s, I was spotted by Tim Crimp, a scout from Watford FC, who were then in the equivalent of the Championship League. He invited me to a local trial which Watford FC were holding in the area. I was then invited to go to the Hornets for their summer schools. They only selected two of us from that south-west trial. The other player was Paul Jennings, who happened to be a good friend of mine since our youth. I remember the great feeling I had on opening the letter and seeing the headed notepaper with the Watford crest at the top.

Every summer holiday and during the half-terms, Paul and I would make the train journey to Watford for their football training schools. I think I grew up very quickly during those sessions, and it was fantastic to receive such top coaching. Everything at Vicarage Road was at a different level from what I was used to; it was a professional club with professional coaches. During the second Watford summer school Paul and I stayed in Kenny Jackett's house for the week. Kenny was the first-team coach at the time. Maybe I made a good impression on him. I was not to know then that our paths would cross later in my career at Swansea City. That second summer at Vicarage Road was an important time, as the youth coach, Stuart Murdoch, told us that some of us would be offered YTS (Youth Training Scheme) contracts.

Twelve of us sat anxiously in a room waiting to be called in to see Stuart. Five had gone in looking nervous, and had come out all smiles as they had been offered contracts.

It was now my turn to chat with Stuart. But I came

out looking as glum as I had gone in. Watford didn't want me. I then had to stay in the room and watch the other six go in for their meeting. They were all signed up by the club. I was the only one who wasn't. It was horrible watching their happy faces and it was difficult going back on the train to Torquay with my friend Paul Jennings. He was obviously thrilled, but was trying not to show it. I was gutted, but was trying not to let Paul see my disappointment because I was also happy for him.

When I got back I just cried my eyes out to my mum and dad. I couldn't believe I was the only one not to be offered a contract. I felt crushed. But that was the springboard for me as I ended up signing for Torquay United FC as a YTS player on a two-year contract in 1995–6. I made my professional debut, aged 16, at Sealand Road away to Chester City, whilst still a youth team player. I was very pleased with my performance and marked Cyrille Regis. It was very much a baptism of fire, marking an ex-international who had scored over 130 goals at the highest level for West Bromwich Albion, Aston Villa and Coventry City.

The manager at Torquay United's Plainmoor ground was Eddie May, a giant of a man who made his name as a centre-half for Southend United, Wrexham and Swansea City. In his time at the Racecourse, he had the distinction of scoring 35 goals for the club with his head. Before becoming manager of Torquay United, he had been coach at Leicester City under the legendary Jock Wallace, and had helped them to the Second Division title (now known as the Championship League). Eddie showed great belief in me by giving me my chance in only the first year of my youth team contract. Since finishing writing this book, I've been saddened to hear that Eddie passed away on 14 April 2012. He was a great man who will be sorely missed by everyone who knew him.

That year, 1995–6, I was also selected to play for England under-16s. It was a great honour, especially as many of the players in the squad were on the books of Premiership sides. I was told to report for training at England's training base in Lilleshall. Paul Compton and Kevin Hodges, who were my youth team coaches and were massive influences on my development at Torquay, impressed on me that I shouldn't turn up in my scruffs. So, my mum spent days preparing and sewing a Torquay United badge onto a smart blazer. When I arrived at Lilleshall, I didn't know any of the other players or coaching staff. Walking into the meeting room for the first time, I saw that all the other players were in jeans and casual tops – it was so embarrassing! I was devastated. Mark Gower, who is now my team mate at Swansea City, was in the squad as a Tottenham Hotspur player. He has never allowed me to forget that incident and, even to this day when we turn up for training and games, he will sometimes turn to me and say, 'Have you remembered your blazer Garry?'

Coming from a team in the bottom division of the Football League, it was great to train with such talented players. In addition to Mark Gower, also in the squad were: Rio Ferdinand, England and Manchester United stalwart; Jody Morris, former Chelsea player; and John Curtis, who went on to play for Aston Villa, Derby County and helped Leicester

City into the Championship. I roomed with Jeff Whitley, who played for Manchester City. Although I didn't play in a full international, I did play one game against a British Universities XI, which was a great experience, one in which I felt I did well whilst also earning the respect of those players by the end of the week's training.

When I got back to Torquay I turned out for the first team a few more times, making a total of five first-team appearances towards the end of the 1995–6 season. It was a difficult season for the Gulls and we struggled throughout, finishing bottom of the division. We should have been relegated but Stevenage Borough, who won the Conference League, were not promoted because their ground did not comply with Football League standards. This meant that Torquay United remained a Football League club.

At the end of that season, Southampton, who were then a Premiership team, asked my club's permission for me to join them on a summer youth team tour of Germany. They were taking part in a mini-tournament with Frankfurt, Hadjuk Split of Yugoslavia, Bayern Munich and a couple of other German teams. I was fortunate to play in all the games and was pleased with my performances. I think some of the regular youth players from the Saints were wondering, 'Who is this guy?' No doubt, they felt they should have been playing instead of me, especially those who played in my position of defender. In the first game we beat favourites Bayern Munich 2–0, and then drew with Frankfurt and beat Borussia Dortmund 3–1 in our final round-robin game. In the semi-final we faced Hadjuk Split and the game finished a goalless draw at the end of the 90 minutes and extra time. Matt Oakley (who went on to play many Premiership games for the Saints) missed the crucial penalty and we lost the penalty shoot-out. We then defeated Frankfurt to finish third in the tournament.

I enjoyed the trip, although I could have done without the 30-hour coach journey there and back! Dennis Rofe, the youth team coach at Southampton, chatted with me and told me that he and the rest of the coaching staff had been very pleased with my performances in the tournament. He said that they were going to monitor my progress at Torquay during the following season. After finishing bottom of the division, Torquay sacked manager Eddie May that summer, and promoted my youth team coaches, Paul Compton and Kevin Hodges, to joint managers. When I told them what Dennis Rofe had said, they encouraged me by saying that if I stayed at Torquay, I would play regularly for the first team in the coming season.

That summer I went away with some of my friends on my first ever lads' holiday. We went to Ibiza and had a great time. On the last night we were in a nightclub when I got a telephone message from Paul Compton telling me that Southampton wanted to sign me. I suppose I should have been over the moon but, to my surprise, I was actually devastated! It would mean me leaving my family and lots of my friends who were playing for Torquay United with me, and I really didn't want to go.

When I got back home I chatted with the club chairman, Mike Bateson, and my coaches Paul and

Kevin. Slowly it dawned on me what I was being offered. I was currently on the books of a club that, if it weren't for the state of Stevenage Borough's ground, would be in the Conference League. Southampton were offering to pay £200,000 for me with add ons if I made the grade. I had the chance of becoming a Premiership footballer.

My mother and father drove me to the Dell to meet the Southampton management. We were met by Lawrie McMenemy, who was head of football development there at the time, a massive, imposing figure of a man. He told us that the Saints would take over my YTS contract for its final year and that I would be given a two-year professional contract after that on a wage of £200. The second year's wage would rise to £220 a week. In those days there weren't many agents in football, and my parents and I were too much in awe of Lawrie and the whole set-up at the Dell to argue for more money. Besides, my parents were not skilled financial negotiators. But none of that mattered, as I was signing for a Premier League football club and, for the next seven years, had the best football education I could ever have asked for.

I will never forget my first week as a Southampton player. Partly because I was suddenly surrounded in the youth team by talented players, such as Wayne Bridge who was to go on and play at the highest level for England and club sides such as Chelsea and Manchester City. The other unforgettable moment that week came one afternoon when we had been put through our paces. Our coach, Alan Mullery, suggested we move to the other pitch and watch the first team stars in action. We hadn't been on the touchline for long when Graeme Souness, the Saints' manager at the time, and Dave Beasant, the ex-Wimbledon goalkeeper, famous for his FA Cup final heroics against Liverpool, were playing in a five-a-side game and both clashed in a tackle, leading to a throwing of a few punches before being split up. A little later in the same game, Robbie Slater, an Australian international, and Alan Neilson fell out. Neilson used his two fingers to poke Slater in the eyes which also led to them scuffling before being torn apart. Not quite what our youth team coach had in mind for us to be watching I'm sure.

The youth team in which I played was in the Premier Youth League. It meant that I was often pitting my wits against players who were to make it big in the future. The Leeds team we faced had players such as Jonathan Woodgate, Alan Smith and Harry Kewell. In spite of that, we beat them 7–1 in a game at Staplewood (Southampton's training ground). Incidentally, the next time I played against Alan Smith was two seasons ago, when we were playing Newcastle United at the Liberty Stadium. Alan played for the Magpies and captained the team. Before going into the referee's room prior to the game, I asked Alan how he was and wished him good luck for the game. He turned to me and said, 'As long as we don't get done like the last time we played against each other, I'll be happy.' I was impressed that he remembered all those years later.

As a YTS player, I was assigned two first-team players to look after. I was basically their gopher. One was Paul Tisdale, who has gone on to do so well as manager of Exeter City and, at one time, was seriously considered by Swansea City as a successor to Paulo Sousa. Paul was a great character and I enjoyed looking after him! I'm afraid I can't say the same for the other one, Simon Charlton. He moaned about everything; part of my duties was to prepare my two pro's training kits every day. In the winter, when I had to lay out Simon's kit, I'd have to wait and watch as he pulled up in the car park, then rush to get his kit into the tumble dryer so it was all laid out and still warm before he made it into the changing rooms. Perhaps he was trying to teach me, or harden me up for a life as a professional, who knows? He would ask me to clean the white strips on his black boots with a Jiff cleaner. It was nearly impossible to get them completely white and took forever to do each day. On one particular day, I had cleaned his boots ready to be packed for the first team's match at the weekend but Andrew Sullivan, another youth team player whose job was to pack the boot skip, forgot to put Charlton's boots in (and unbeknown to me). Southampton were playing away at Blackburn and I can remember watching the game on Sky TV. Suddenly, Simon Charlton appears on the screen wearing red boots. What's he doing, I thought to myself. He hasn't got red boots. They must be new.

When Simon arrived at training the following Monday he called me into the dressing room and just unleashed a barrage of abuse in my direction in front of the entire first-team squad. I had to stand there quietly and take it all on the chin, but really I just wanted to punch him in the face.

Alan Mullery, the youth coach, told me that I would be in trouble. I realized I was heading for 'Jimmy's

Revenge'. This punishment consisted of eight bricks having to be carried from the starting line of a 40-metre long grid, which was split up into five 8-metre intervals. Sprinting as fast as possible, you had to pick up a brick and take it to the first 8-metre line, then a second brick to the 16-metre line, then another to the 24-metre line and so on. If that wasn't hard enough, you then had to retrieve each brick, one at a time, and return it to the start line. If you failed to finish within a certain time, you would have to do it all again. Trust me, this was a very painful experience. All I could think of was smashing Simon Charlton's face in to get me through it.

During my time at Southampton I saw Graeme Souness replaced by Dave Jones; he would give me my Premiership debut, aged 19 years, at the Dell against a Derby County team that included talented players such as Paulo Wanchope and Dean Sturridge. I could never have imagined at the time that Dave would eventually become manager of Cardiff City and become a fierce rival. Sadly for Dave, he lost his job because of an ongoing court case; he was accused of abusing children at the children's home where he had worked during the 1980s. The accusations were later proved to be groundless, but it was a very difficult time for him and his family. I felt it was a shame that Dave wasn't given more backing by Southampton, as he was sacked before a verdict had even been given.

Jones was replaced by Glenn Hoddle, which was at the time when news was starting to break about how he was being influenced by the Christian guru Eileen Drury. On one occasion, playing away to Tranmere Rovers in the League Cup, the Saints had been 3–0 up at Prenton Park, but somehow managed to lose the game 4–3. The players knew that there would be an inquest into what happened. The following day, Matt Le Tissier and Dean Richards and a few others entered into a bet to see who could get the word 'God' into the post-match discussion. So, the whole squad sat in a meeting room, with Glenn Hoddle addressing all the players and asking for their thoughts. Dean Richards was the first to speak. 'A really bad result,' he said 'we were three up and then the first Tranmere goal went in, then the second. The only way I can describe it is to say it felt as if there was some sort of spirit. It was as if God or some sort of powerful force was coming down against us.'

All of us wanted to burst out laughing; we couldn't believe that Deano had actually said it. So, as we were all trying to hide our faces, to our amazement Glenn nodded and said, 'You know it's funny you should say that Deano, I felt exactly the same.' Wow, we couldn't believe it, we all thought Hoddle would think it was taking the mickey. Dean Richards cleaned up whatever money was on the bet!

Although lots of people had misgivings about Hoddle's judgement and the influence of Eileen Drury, from a coaching point of view he was absolutely brilliant. During one training session we were doing crossing and shooting. Individual players would stand in the middle of the pitch and then have to send passes out to wingers on the right and left flanks who would then do a combination to get a cross in for the attackers inside the 18-yard box to finish on goal. Hoddle was obviously getting annoyed at how inaccurate everyone was with their passes out to the wingers. He stopped the session and stepped up to the middle, took the ball and pinged perfect balls to the right and then the left wing using both feet. The passes were inch perfect, rising barely a couple inches off the floor straight to their intended targets. It was the best demonstration of passing I've ever seen. The lesson over, he then asked next in line Chris Marsden to restart the session and show what he had just witnessed. Marsden obliged by blasting his pass over the winger's head and into the bushes, leaving the boys to laugh under their breath and Hoddle shaking his head in anger.

After Glenn Hoddle left Southampton for Tottenham Hotspur, he was replaced by Gordon Strachan. I was 23 years old at the start of Gordon's first season and I will never forget our pre-season training. Gordon took the squad up to Scotland. I think it's the hardest training I've ever done in my football career. But, despite the physical strain, I enjoyed it immensely. Gordon Strachan liked me and told me that he wanted me to have more experience. He asked me to sign a new contract and I was quite often on the bench and in and around the first-team squad.

During my time at Southampton I was also sometimes loaned out to clubs such as Sheffield Wednesday, Oxford United, Stockport County and Torquay United. Funnily enough, when I went to Sheffield Wednesday, Swansea had enquired about getting me on loan as well. Unbeknown to me at the time, Swansea were in a real relegation scrap. It was the 2002–3 season, when Swansea famously beat Hull City in the last game of that season to remain in the Football League. If I'd known what I know now, I would have loved to have come to help the cause, but thankfully it turned out alright in the end.

When I was on loan at Sheffield I had a phone call from Kevin Davies, who was a player at Southampton but had been brought up in Sheffield. He told me that he was in Sheffield for the night and that he was going to a bar in the city centre with Chris Waddle whom I knew when we were both on loan at Torquay United. I met them for about 30 minutes, then made my way back to my hotel. The next day I was called into the office by the Sheffield manager, Chris Turner. I was in the doghouse, as he told me that players were banned from going into any pubs, bars or clubs in the town centre at night due to a previous players' night out ending up with some of them getting into a fight. I told Chris I wasn't aware of that, and that I had only gone into the bar to have a quick chat with Davies and Waddle. Turner told me that rules were rules, and that he had already rung Gordon Strachan to ask if it was OK to fine me. I couldn't believe Chris Turner hadn't spoken to me first; now I had Gordon Strachan believing that I was out on the lash on a night out. And if that wasn't bad enough, I knew Strachan was fiercely opposed to his players drinking.

From then on Gordon Strachan's attitude towards me changed. When I returned to Southampton I tried to explain, but the damage was done. It was very disappointing, especially as everyone else in the management team told me how well I was doing. It was the season when Southampton had a wonderful run in the FA Cup and reached the final where they would meet Arsenal. A few weeks before the final, the tailors arrived at the Dell for a suit-fitting exercise for the squad. I couldn't understand why I was being measured, as I was convinced I wouldn't be involved in the final because I had not been involved in any first-team squads for some time. The senior players told me that everyone was to have a suit, although I wondered why. A few days later, when the tailors had made all the suits, we were called to the St Mary's Stadium to try them on and line up for the team photo. I was trying my suit on in the dressing room when, out the corner of my eye, I saw Gordon Strachan standing behind me pulling silly faces at me in front of some of the senior players, as if to say what is he doing having a suit. I spun around and asked him 'Have you got a problem?' He then just tried to laugh it off, so I said 'you're taking the piss, I don't even want to be here and didn't even want this suit'. I felt good that I had stood up to him. I wasn't going to be made a fool of.

Despite the fact that things became difficult towards the end of my time at the Dell, I have some wonderful memories of my time there, especially of the games in which I featured. I was very lucky that many of my Premiership appearances for Southampton were against some of the big teams. Playing in the 2–1 win against Manchester United, I defended against Quinton Fortune and Ryan Giggs while, in the match with Newcastle United I marked the legendary Alan Shearer and his strike partner Duncan Ferguson. One memory which sticks with me from that game was when I tackled Ferguson and accidentally caught him on the ankle. As I jogged to the centre circle, I could tell he was angry and he stared at me, a pretty chilling feeling, trust me. Nine players out of ten would have said something to me, but Ferguson remained silent. Towards the end of the game, Duncan showed that he hadn't forgotten. As I was defending in my penalty area, he steamed into the penalty box at the far post, crashed into me and flattened me. Just to remind me that I might be a young lad, but this was a man's game.

Against Liverpool I was thrilled to be playing on the same pitch as players such as Michael Owen, Robbie Fowler and John Barnes. We were absolutely hammered and lost 1–7. I can remember coming off the pitch and sitting in the dressing room. That was the worst I've ever felt after any match. Now, before every game I remind myself of how I felt after that defeat. I make a promise to myself that I will never let that feeling happen to me again in my playing career. I never want to experience that sheer embarrassment again. I will go down fighting.

I was lucky enough to play in the last league game at the Dell before the Saints moved to St Mary's Stadium. We were drawing 2–2 against Arsenal and Matt Le Tissier came off the bench to score the winning goal – you couldn't have written a better script. I marked the likes of Robert Pires and Thierry Henry and the atmosphere that day was absolutely incredible. The crowd of 15,000 plus made themselves sound more like 40,000. When Matt's shot hit the back of the net, the noise of the crowd's roar was the loudest I had ever heard. That was such an important victory for us, saying goodbye to the Dell – it was great for everyone to leave the place on a high.

It was brilliant to play with players as amazing as Matt Le Tissier. As far as I am concerned, he is the best player I have ever played with. The man was a magician who could do anything he wanted with the ball. Chelsea were keen on him at one time, but he refused to move as he was happy at the south coast club. It was a good time for me. Rubbing shoulders with players of the calibre of Andrei Kanchelskis, Dan Petrescu, Mark Hughes, David Hirst, Carlton Palmer, Dean Richards and Claus Lundekvam to mention but a few, plus great young stars such as Kevin Davies, James Beattie and Wayne Bridge. I learned so much. I didn't play for the first team as often as I could have wished for, but the experiences I had certainly added to my football education.

Southampton taught me how to play football. My only regret was that I didn't leave a couple years earlier, as I felt they were a little wasted.

Five months before my contract ran out at Southampton, I was sent to Barnsley. I signed on loan for the Tykes in November 2003. I made my debut for them in a goalless draw in the FA Cup at Ashton Gate against Bristol City. I made a further 14 appearances for them before I was injured in a game at Blundell Park, away to Grimsby Town towards the end of March, with only two months of the season remaining. Everyone seemed pleased with my performances since I'd arrived. So much so that the chairman, Peter Ridsdale, told me and my agent that at the end of the season, I would be offered a two-year contract. During this time I was sidelined by my ankle injury, and manager Gudjon Thordason was sacked, with Paul Hart replacing him until the end of the season. At the same time I had seen a house in the area which I was interested in buying. I contacted Peter Ridsdale and explained the situation, as I wanted to check that the promise of the contract still held. He told me that everything was fine, so I went ahead and put a deposit of £5,000 down on the house.

At the end of the season there were nine players at the club who were out of contract. I was called into the manager's office to see Paul Hart and Peter Ridsdale, thinking it would just be a formality and that Barnsley would be offering me my new contract. Paul Hart told me, 'You have been injured, so I haven't seen much of you since I've been here, so I am afraid I will not be offering you a contract.'

I was absolutely stunned, and fuming at the same time. Not only was I now without a club, but I was also in the terrible position of losing my non-refundable deposit on the house which I would no longer be buying. I stood up and looked towards Peter Ridsdale. I stared at him, but he wouldn't look me in the eye. 'You're a joke,' I told him. 'An absolute disgrace.'

A week later, Kenny Jackett who of course had known me from the summer training sessions at Watford, contacted me. In the middle of the previous season he had taken over from Brian Flynn at the Vetch in Swansea, and he was asking me to join the club. I liked the thought of teaming up with Kenny again, but I wasn't keen on playing League Two football as I thought I was good enough to play in a higher division, but I agreed to go down and meet him and have a look at the club.

Chapter Two

I MUST ADMIT that when I first drove to Swansea for that initial chat with the club, I had never been to the city in my life. I had no idea where in south Wales it was and, as I by-passed Port Talbot, I looked down and saw what I now know to be Aberavon Rugby Club. I thought, please God no, that can't be the Vetch Field. Not only was I confused by the ground, but I was also confused by the Welsh signs. I kept seeing pointers to Abertawe and, as I didn't know it was Welsh for Swansea, I thought I'd carry on driving. After driving for a while longer, I thought I'd gone too far, so I did an about turn and ended up in Llanelli, where someone told me that Abertawe and Swansea were one and the same.

My visit to Swansea was made easier by the fact that Adrian Forbes and Sam Ricketts were also looking around the city with a view to joining the club. I had got to know Sam a little when I was on loan at Oxford United, and I'd played against Forbes just a few weeks earlier when I'd been on loan at Barnsley and we played Luton. After chatting, I knew I would get on well with both of them and it was good to be in a new place with two other people. Two things impressed me about my visit to Swansea.

It was clear after speaking to Kenny that he had a clear vision and really wanted the squad to progress. Secondly, although the club played at the Vetch, we were told all about the plans for the Liberty Stadium. We were given a tour of the new site, saw the shell of the stadium and realized that this would help the club to move forward also. I went home that evening and took a couple days to talk things through with my family. I had a few other clubs interested, but nothing as concrete as Swansea and, after the good feeling I'd had after my visit to the city, it was an easy decision.

I signed for the Swans and was allowed to miss the first week of training so that I could go to Southampton to sort things out before moving to my new home in Swansea. When I joined up with the players on the following Monday, it became clear that whilst I was away in Southampton the boys had been out for a drink the Sunday night at a bar called The Lounge on Wind Street. They'd got into an argument with the staff over a bottle of peach schnapps. This meant that my first encounter with my new team mates would be a disciplinary meeting. Kenny Jackett had heard reports about the arguments and was not too pleased as it was also well known that there was a bit of a drinking culture at the club from previous seasons – something which Kenny wanted to stamp out. 'What the hell went on?' he wanted to know.

Andy Robinson was the first to speak up and explained that a week earlier, they had bought bottles of peach schnapps at the same bar for half the price. I couldn't help smiling. Robbo and the boys really seemed to be missing the point, but they were all outraged at the increase in price in the space of a few days. Kenny also pointed out that the actual issue was different. 'You're all moaning about how much this bloody bottle is when the fact is you all shouldn't be out on the town drinking just before training anyway lads.' He decided to ban us all from Wind Street, the main area for wine bars and pubs in Swansea. At this point Lee Trundle interrupted and spoke for all the other players. 'Boss, you can't take that away from us, we have no place else to go,' he said. I couldn't believe Trunds was seriously telling the boss this! But, over the years, I've become great friends with Lee and know how much he loves his nights out! The gaffer eventually retracted the ban, but I think he had made his point. Although I found the whole incident amusing, I have to admit I was impressed by the way the boys fought for each other. It showed me that they were a close-knit unit.

The 2004–5 season was a very important and emotional one for the Swans fans, as it was the last season we would be playing at the Vetch Field before moving to our new stadium. My first game for the Swans was the opening match of the season at the Vetch, against Northampton Town. Although we lost 0–2, I was pleased with my performance. Sam Ricketts also made his debut, and I think we were both amazed by the passion of the fans. The noise they made banging the corrugated back of the North Bank was incredible. Any opposing defender or winger on that side of the pitch must have found the atmosphere really intimidating. The season was to prove a very eventful and enjoyable one for me.

In early October we drew 1–1 at Chester City. I was

marking their striker Cortez Belle, a big lump of a lad. During the game, he and I started to run for the same ball. He pushed me from behind and, as I fell, he kneed me accidentally in the face. I was knocked out cold. I would end up needing ten stitches to a nasty cut inside my mouth. I was carried off and taken to the physician's room. One of my lasting memories of that incident is looking across the physician's room and seeing Cortez Belle – he was lying down on one of the other medical beds. He seemed to be rubbing his knee and saying to one of his physios 'Ouch, my knee is really hurting.' I couldn't believe it! There I was, going in and out of consciousness and all that Cortez was worried about was his knee which had caused all the damage! And there was I thinking he had come to see how I was and to say how sorry he was!

In that season I was sent off three times. Perhaps the most memorable dismissal was at Gay Meadow, playing against Shrewsbury Town in November. Early on in the game I was booked for splitting up a potential scuffle between our big Kevin Austin and a Shrewsbury player as they seemed to be going head to head. The linesman flagged the referee and told him to caution me for pushing, which was just laughable. Ten minutes later I tackled their player Luke Rodgers near touch on the halfway line. I got a slight feel on the ball with my studs as he jumped over my outstretched leg whilst the ball rolled out of play for a throw-in. Both of us just jogged back into position to wait for the throw-in to be taken but, as I turned, I saw referee Eddie Evans running towards me reaching for his pocket, pulling out first a yellow, then his red card as he arrived right in front of me. I couldn't believe the decision. I was incensed. I will be the first to admit that what happened next was not acceptable and the way to react but, as the red mist came down, I was in his face shouting, 'You're a disgrace, that wasn't even a foul.' Of course there were a few other choice words being said too. But as I shared my views with him, he was walking backwards, probably trying to avoid the froth from my mouth. Then he tripped and fell over. I suppose from the terraces it looked as if I had headbutted him. In no time at all, five or six stewards were on the pitch, players from both sides were all around pushing and shoving. As I left the pitch, three stewards met me at the entrance to the tunnel and had their hands on me as they tried to lead me towards the dressing room.

When we walked through the tunnel I had lost all sense of calm. I was still absolutely furious about what had just happened. I told the stewards, in no uncertain terms, to take their hands off of me, and they keenly obliged. When I approached the dressing room door I kicked it as hard as I could. Instead of swinging open like a western saloon door, it slipped off its hinges. Still fuming, I started hurtling the plastic containers of protein shakes, and anything I could get my hands on, in the direction of these three stewards as they were struggling to put the door back on. But, sensing my mood, they beat a hasty retreat.

Just a few minutes into my time in the dressing room, I heard a commotion coming from the tunnel. I heard this loud thud against the dressing room door and, for the second time in a few minutes, the door totally came off its hinges – this time in an irreparable state. Andy Robinson came storming into the room – he had been sent off as well. He was flanked by the same stewards who had led me off the field. Andy also went straight for whatever he could lay his hands on to throw at the stewards. I have to admit that I began to feel rather sorry for them. This time they decided against trying to fix the door. I think they thought that between the two of us there was far too much anger and danger around the place. They beat another hasty retreat.

Andy sat down next to me. After a few minutes of silence, we had calmed down. We caught each other's eyes and, as I explained about the door, both of us started laughing at the situation we were in and what had just happened with those stewards. I suppose it was at that moment we began to realize what fools we'd been and also what trouble we would be in. I was given an automatic two-game ban because I had already received a red card earlier in the season. Kenny decided to appeal against the ban.

The following week I was called before the Football Association of Wales in Cardiff, where they were trying to charge me with assault. We decided to appeal against all the charges, especially as the referee Eddie Evans's report stated I had not touched him and that he had tripped and fallen over. It even said I had not sworn at him! So we believed we had a very strong case. Kenny Jackett and the club chairman, Huw Jenkins, came with me to the hearing. It was extraordinary that not one member of the appeal panel had actually seen the incident on video. In my defence Kenny showed them a video of what had actually happened, confident that it would be clear to see neither incident warranted a yellow card, thus rescinding the red card and the ban. After our case was put forward, the three of us were asked to sit outside the room and they told us they would call us back in once they had made their decision.

While we were waiting I saw a large tray piled with sandwiches and drinks being taken in for members of the panel and the referee. Thirty minutes later even more food was taken in. Needless to say, we weren't offered any food.

A full hour after the hearing we were called back into the room. In spite of the video evidence and the ref's statement, they decided to drop the assault charge, but turned in a guilty verdict for technical assault (what the hell does that mean?). That was just pathetic from the panel. So, on top of the two-game ban which I had automatically received, the panel gave me a further three-game ban, plus another one for the failed appeal. So, six games in total. When he heard the verdict, Kenny Jackett came out with what I still consider the funniest statement a manager could have made at that moment. He looked at them all behind their table and said, 'If I were Ian Holloway (the Blackpool manager), I suppose I would say, "It feels like we've all been abducted by aliens and we're having this meeting on Mars."' I suddenly remembered that I had been told that if I lost the hearing I would have to pay the expenses of the tribunal. That meant that those two mountains of sandwiches which had passed us in the corridor had been paid for by me. Technically these were my sandwiches. So, as I stood up and left Kenny and Huw to argue the verdict with the panel, I thought to myself, bugger them, they've just found me guilty of something I didn't do, so they're not having any more to eat. I went over to the sandwiches and marched out of the room carrying them in my hands, followed by a few of the FAW administration staff. They asked me, 'What are you doing with them?' 'Chucking them in the bin!' I replied. 'You can't do that.' 'Watch me,' I said and once outside the room, I threw them all in the bin.

Looking back at it now I think it was all a bit of a stitch up. I mean, what kind of panel comes to an appeal meeting and has not even watched the incidents to be discussed or even brought a video of the game with them. This proved to me they had already made a predetermined decision without hearing my appeal. I was also told afterwards that some members of the panel were from Cardiff, and we were in Cardiff. Make of that what you will! In all I served a suspension of ten games that season for the three red cards, something that I wasn't proud of and needed to learn my lessons from.

I suppose every football season has defining games for every team. When you look back there are certain games which were more significant than others and they were the crucial ones to try and win. In the 2004–5 season, I would say that the important ones were against Bristol Rovers, Yeovil Town and Macclesfield, all at the Vetch. The match against Bristol Rovers was in early November, just a couple of weeks before that fateful game at Gay Meadow against Shrewsbury. Against Bristol Rovers there was a great atmosphere as nearly 9,000 fans crammed into the ground. It was a very hard-fought game, and with two minutes to go there was no score and the game seemed to be heading for a goalless draw. Then, we were awarded a penalty. Lee Trundle took it and missed, but was then controversially ordered to retake it because the referee believed that some of the Rovers' players had encroached into the penalty area, which incensed the Rovers manager and players. He scored from the retake and sent the Jack Army wild. I remember Andy Gurney standing right in front of the Rovers' fans celebrating and goading them. Not the brightest thing to do, being a former Rovers player himself, being a Bristol boy, and also living there and commuting to Swansea every day. I think he didn't go back for a month after that game as he thought he would be lynched.

For the Yeovil match the attendance was over 11,000 which, at that stage, was the highest in League Two for that season. It was always a massive game against Yeovil, as they were chasing promotion as well, and were a very good team at that level. Paul Connor scored for us, but the goal was disallowed and then, in the last ten minutes, Yeovil scored twice to beat us 0–2.

I've already mentioned the incredible atmosphere at the Vetch but, for some reason, it was always extra special for night matches. Our game against Macclesfield was on Good Friday evening. Macclesfield were chasing us for promotion and nearly 10,000 fans turned out for the game. The atmosphere created by the fans before kick-off was amazing and they kept up the noise levels right to the end of the game. We went 2–0 ahead after goals by Lee Thorpe and Paul Connor and, although

Macclesfield came at us late on, we saw the game out comfortably. We completed a good Easter with an away win at Cheltenham then, after a 3–0 home win against Cambridge United, we suffered a real hammer blow with a 0–1 defeat at Lincoln, where I scored the most bizarre own goal I have ever scored. Andy Robinson was taking too long to clear the ball by the touchline ten yards from our own 18-yard box. He turned back inside and miskicked his clearance and sent the ball flying towards me, as I was stood facing their goal on my 18-yard line. As I tried to make a good connection, I scuffed the floor and the ball looped straight up into the air. With the spin and strong wind, the ball looped back and went into the far top corner of our goal. I couldn't do that again if I tried. We then got back on track with a 1–0 home victory over Oxford United, in front of a 10,602 crowd.

Our next game was away to Bristol Rovers, where we lost 0–2 and had Andy Robinson sent off just before half-time (if you get a chance to watch that sending off on YouTube then do, as it's very amusing watching Robbo's tantrum whilst leaving the pitch). That defeat left us two points away from automatic promotion. There were two games left for us so that we could win promotion to League One: Shrewsbury at home and Bury at Gigg Lane. They both turned out to be really memorable games.

Our fixture against the Shrews was to be the last league game ever played at the Vetch, as the Liberty Stadium was ready for us to use in the next season. The build-up to this game was enormous, with huge media interest in the fact that the club had played at the same stadium for 93 years. In the days leading up to the game, there were functions and auctions with special videos and books being produced. On the match day itself, there were marquees around the ground. It was more like a carnival atmosphere than a football match. It was all great for the fans but, as players, we knew we had to focus on an important match, and we found it hard to relax. From inside the dressing room we could hear the excitement on the pitch. Before kick-off, stars of earlier Swansea teams paraded around the ground. The entertainer Max Boyce and Katherine Jenkins sang for the crowd and there was even a wedding. Kevin Johns, who does all the pre-match announcing for the Swans, officiated at the wedding of mascots Cyril and Sybil the swans!

When we walked onto the pitch the noise created by the fans was unbelievable. The attendance that day was 11,469, and we had hoped that it would be the record attendance for League Two in the 2004–5 season. Unfortunately, we were pipped by the crowd at Roots Hall, where 11,735 turned up for the top-of-the-table clash between Southend United and Yeovil.

The game was difficult, possibly because of the atmosphere and the high expectation of the crowd. After a nervy start, thankfully Adrian Forbes scored against a certain Paul Hart, who is now Manchester City and England's number one goalkeeper, which also proved to be the only goal of the match. In the end we had to thank our goalie, Willy Gueret, for keeping us in the game with some fabulous saves. It was great to leave the Vetch on such an emotional high, and give the old place the send off it deserved. The all-important three points nudged us nearer and nearer to the possibility of promotion.

The final game was at Gigg Lane, away to Bury. The home team were safe in mid-table, whereas we had everything to play for. As we drove to Bury, we knew that our team and Southend United could join Yeovil and Scunthorpe and finish in the last automatic place. We needed to win and hope that Southend would draw or lose. With a crowd of 7,575, including 4,608 travelling fans from Swansea, the atmosphere was amazing – it felt like a home game. After 27 seconds Adrian Forbes gave the travelling Jack Army something to celebrate when he put us in the lead. About 200 fans ran on to the pitch in wild celebration, jumping on all the boys. They kept coming on to the pitch throughout the game. With ten minutes left we were still up 1–0. The referee stopped the game and told us, 'If your fans don't stop coming over the barriers, I'm going to abandon the game.' Bury's captain wanted his team to walk off the pitch. We were all furious and started arguing with their players. We couldn't understand why they were doing this. Did they all have friends playing for Southend? Andy Gurney, who was a substitute, walked straight up to their captain and told him if he didn't get back on the pitch straight away, he'd be getting a bit of a slap. Both benches had a bit of a coming together. Lee Trundle, who had been substituted with 20 minutes remaining, was told by Kenny Jackett to go and calm the fans down so that the game wouldn't be stopped. Lee walked round in front of our fans, pleading with them to remain behind the barriers. Eventually, order was restored.

Because of the delays, word had got round to us on the pitch that the Southend game had finished, and that they had lost. So we only needed to hold on to our one goal lead. We played out a very tense and nervous final ten minutes with the Bury team frantically throwing extra men forward in search of an equalizer. Again, we couldn't believe it. I was asking one of their centre halves why he and others were now staying up front when the game didn't mean anything to them, but he just shrugged his shoulders. This made us even more determined. We managed to hold on. When the final whistle was blown, it sparked wild scenes. Thousands of our fans swarmed onto the pitch to celebrate. We all had to make a mad dash to get into the tunnel or risk being trampled.

Once outside the dressing rooms, all of us were so happy but also furious about the way the Bury team had behaved. Because we were so annoyed, we decided to rub their noses in it by celebrating outside their dressing room. I don't think they fancied coming out, as we had some big boys in our team, plus Leon Britton who could bite their ankles off. We soon turned our attentions back to celebrating. We went up into the stand to see our fans who were still dancing and chanting ecstatically on the grass underneath where we were standing. I say standing, but the stand and the director's box were so small that we were all completely crammed in. The police started pushing the fans and the players, but we had nowhere to go or move to. It was chaos. One officer tried to push Willy Gueret to one side. But Willy is a big strong fellow, and he stood his ground. Because they couldn't move him, the police decided to arrest him, but it took four officers to prise his hands together. 'Don't make him angry, he's French and very moody,' I told the police, trying to make them lighten up a bit – but they didn't take any notice. After the game several of the fans told us that the police had been very heavy-handed with them. Some had found it terrifying, especially as there were many young fans among them and police charging them on horseback and others letting dogs off their leads.

Back in the dressing room there were manic celebrations. We were all so excited as, just two seasons earlier, Swansea City had been in danger of going out of the league, and now here we were heading for League One. When we eventually got back on the team bus, Kenny Jackett came to the back and said to us, 'Well done boys. It's been a brilliant season. Our next game is against Wrexham in the Welsh Cup final on Tuesday, so don't go mad tonight.' I think we all looked at each other and everyone shouted at the same time 'Shut up gaffer, we're getting smashed!' We laughed and Kenny laughed too.

Despite all the joy in that dressing room, there was one little problem. Or should I say one big problem? Willy Gueret. He had been taken to the local police station. So we now had to make the decision whether to leave him up north and let him get back down to Swansea in a taxi, or wait for him with the team bus. It showed the solidarity of the team that we all agreed we should wait. We had all done this together and so we wanted Willy to be part of it.

We sat in the team coach outside the police station waiting for his release. From time to time we would beep the bus horn and chant, 'Free Willy, Free Willy'. We knew that his favourite tipple was Jack Daniels, so we had a bottle waiting for him. After waiting for a couple of hours, they released him with just a caution. He got on the bus, but he wasn't terribly communicative and his face was like thunder. As soon as he saw what we had bought him, that face changed into a smile and we enjoyed an amazing bus journey back to south Wales for a weekend of partying.

Despite a happy Saturday night and all day Sunday in the bars of Wind Street, two days later we had a Welsh Premier Cup final against Wrexham to play. I think everyone was still half drunk from the weekend, but somehow we managed to win the game. So, my first season as a Swan ended with promotion and a Cup final victory. That season meant so much to the fans and players. People like Andy Gurney had played in the play-offs five times and had missed out every time. We were such a tight-knit group, partly I think because most of us lived in and around Swansea, not miles away from the ground. This also meant that we formed a bond with the fans. I can't imagine the megastars of Chelsea or Manchester City being as approachable to fans as when we're in local coffee shops or supermarkets, but it happens all the time in Swansea.

So as the 2004–5 season drew to a close, I couldn't wait for 2005–6 season to start. Next stop, the Liberty Stadium and League One.

Chapter Three

Our pre-season training in 2005–6 was at St Athan RAF base. The training was very intense as it was mostly organized for us by the RAF fitness instructors. There are many things I remember from that and what I will never forget is seeing Adebayo Akinfenwa play for the first time after Kenny had signed him from Torquay United. The boys all took minimal clothes for the week, because all we needed were our training kits.

Everyone turned up with small rucksacks, but after waiting for Bayo to meet us all for the first time outside the barracks' canteen, we were gobsmacked to see this massive unit of a man moving towards us with a huge battered suitcase. It had to be the oldest suitcase that was still capable of being moved around. When we saw how tightly it was packed, we all ribbed him and asked whether he was staying on for an extra month! He was so well built, he looked more like an American NFL player than a League One footballer. I think most of the boys were quietly thinking, surely he's not a footballer. But Bayo proved to be a very good player for us and became one of the fans' favourites.

Once he had settled at the club, he also told us

that at that first meeting he had wondered should he smack us all or be nice to us! Thank God it was the latter choice. At lunch the next day, because he was new to the club, he had to do the team initiation which all new players and staff have to do. They have to sing a song of their choice in front of everyone whilst stood on a chair holding a microphone of some description – usually a ketchup bottle or salt shaker. While we were having lunch with all the servicemen from the base, he pulled out his chair, stood on it, shut his eyes and, at the top of his voice, started singing one of the best renditions of Stevie Wonder's 'I just called to say I love you' that I've ever heard! The lad could sing! Just as we'd wondered whether he was a footballer, I'm sure many members of the St Athan's RAF staff were quietly wondering about him and thinking, surely he's not a pilot!

The week's training was very tough. The drill sergeant devised a cycle route for us. Early on, Bayo managed to snap his chain which took 20 minutes to fix. Later, we were all waiting for him at the top of this hill after a gruelling climb. Unbeknown to us, his chain had snapped again. As we looked down the hill, we first saw this bike bouncing around in the air, then, when coming into full view, Bayo was jogging carrying his bike on his shoulders, with assistant manager, Kevin Nugent, puffing away on his bike next to him. I don't know who was more tired, Kevin or Bayo. Bayo was so big and powerful, the bike appeared as if it were the size of a small bag. On the descent there were lots of twists and turns down the country lanes. We were all going at speed. Trunds discovered that his brakes weren't working properly, so he was using his foot on the back wheel to brake. Unfortunatly for Lee, he was going too quickly and was unable to take one corner, so ended up flying head-on into a bush.

Because Lee was at the rear of the group on the descent, all of us had carried on to the bottom before the RAF instructor pulled over to get the group back together for the next phase of the ride. Andy Robinson was the only one who had seen what had happened to Trunds by catching a glimpse behind him. Robbo didn't think of stopping, so when he reached the rest of us he explained what he'd just seen. About five minutes later, a ragged-looking Trunds came rolling into view. He had twigs and leaves in his hair, scratches up his arms and legs. We all just burst out laughing; he looked just like a scarecrow. But Lee was in some discomfort. From what I remember I'm pretty sure he ended up with some broken ribs after the crash.

On one of the days the RAF instructors and Kenny had arranged a paintballing afternoon which was devised to help communication and, most importantly, team bonding. We spent all morning learning various formations and tactics in preparation for the afternoon's paintballing. We were given very strict instructions by the RAF staff on how we should behave. They also showed us how to check the instruments. Sadly, all the tuition was forgotten once we got to the paintball area. Lee Trundle and Andy Robinson decided it would be far more fun to shoot their own team members. Trunds even managed to shoot Roberto Martinez in the crown jewels when he wasn't looking whilst we were all still in the safety area, where shooting your gun was strictly prohibited. The boys were running every way, which way, shouting at the top of their voices, totally disregarding what we had been told in the morning. I just remember looking at the safety area and the RAF staff shaking their heads in disappointment.

Without a doubt, the hardest part of the week's training was running up and down the sand dunes. I have a lasting picture of Bayo struggling. The rest of us were wearing trainers. Bayo had a pair of Nike Air Max boots on, definitely not the right footwear for running, let alone on the sand. I can still clearly picture Colin Pascoe's face pressed on Bayo's bum cheek as he tried to push our new colleague up the last thirty metres of the sand dune.

After the training camp we had a couple of friendlies to look forward to at our new Liberty Stadium, one of which was against Premiership side Fulham, which was also Alan Curtis's testimonial match at which Marc Goodfellow became the first player to score a goal at our new home. We played our first league game at the Liberty Stadium on Saturday, 6 August. Our opponents, Tranmere Rovers, were a good side at this level, and had players that had experience in the higher divisions. They also had players such as Jason McAteer, who had played in the Premiership. Before the curtain-raiser, many fans had been worried whether they would be able to create the same atmosphere as they had at the Vetch. Even as players we wondered how we would cope moving from the cramped playing conditions to the wide open spaces of the new pitch. We knew it would take us a while to feel at home. It takes time to build history at a new venue, for the fans to feel it's their home and give the place a soul. It was our responsibility to try to help the fans make that transition.

We played really well against Tranmere and came out with a 1–0 victory. It was our first game, our first win at the Liberty Stadium and Adebayo Akinfenwa became the first player to score a league goal at the new ground.

Unfortunately, I had to come off at half-time because of ankle ligament damage. While I was sidelined, the boys beat Colchester at Layer Road and followed that with two defeats, including the first loss at our new ground, against Doncaster Rovers (1–2). After slipping out of the League Cup at Reading, we then went on a run of four successive victories. This included the amazing 7–1 thrashing of Bristol City at home. We were all thrilled with that result. We felt that we had really arrived as a club. We could hold our own in a higher league, and were not intimidated by any club who came to our Liberty Stadium, something that was to be a hallmark for the players and the club in the years to come.

I recovered from my injury and then came back into the team for the next game which was a 3–1 win away to MK Dons, with two goals by Andy Robinson, and Lee Trundle getting the other. It was Hartlepool United away next. The match was memorable for the reason that it was the first time that Swansea had flown to an away game in Britain. With 15 minutes left we were leading 2–1 but, despite their late equalizer, we moved to the top of League One.

One game I was particularly disappointed to miss

was the away Football League Trophy match at Plainmoor against Torquay United in mid-October. This was the club where it had all started for me and, of course, my home town. Players always like to go back to their old clubs and try to show what the home fans are missing, so I was gutted not to be in the squad because of illness. My family and friends were also disappointed. It must have affected the attendance, as I'm sure they would have provided most of the crowd!

After getting knocked out of the FA Cup in the first round away to League Two side Stockport County, I returned to defence for the away game at Southend. The game had been billed as the battle between the two hot-shots of League One, Southend's Freddie Eastwood and our own Lee Trundle. Trunds won the battle hands down as we beat the Shrimpers 2–1 and moved to the top of the table.

On the following Friday we played Yeovil at home. It was the first league game played under floodlights at the Liberty Stadium. As I've already mentioned, there was something special about us and evening games. That match was no exception. The atmosphere was electric. I captained the side that night, and Lee Trundle scored two goals to take his tally to 17 in 16 appearances. His second was a wonder strike, when he lobbed the Yeovil keeper from a full 40 metres. That goal, the record crowd of 19,288, and the fact that we had finally defeated our bogey team, meant that it was a fantastic evening. It ended with a female streaker running onto the pitch, which was an added bonus!

A bouncing baby boy at two months old.

Me on the left, aged 4, and my brother Stuart, aged 5.

Now aged 6, with my brother aged 7.

Dressed as a Beaver and Stuart is in a Cub uniform.

Sitting with my mum before playing a match for my school, aged 8.

In my England strip, aged 10.

I was 16 when I signed as an apprentice for Torquay Utd FC.

Awarded Torquay Utd's Young Player of the Year in 1995.

Wearing my Torquay Utd blazer before meeting up with the England under-17s squad. Mark Gower has never let me forget this blazer!

With some of my Torquay Utd team mates on my first lads' holiday in Ibiza.

My first ever car –
a Fiat Uno 60.

Southampton's youth team, 1998/99.

Trying to block a Robbie Fowler shot at Anfield whilst playing for the Saints. We lost 7–1. My worst experience on a football pitch.

Southampton mug shot.

My first game for Southampton's youth team. We beat Reading 4–0.

On loan at Sheffield Wednesday, 2002/03.

With my fiancée, Lexy.

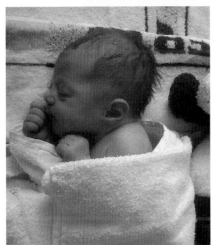

Our new-born daughter, Remy. She's just a few hours old here.

My first ever nappy change – I think it took 30 minutes!

Doing a lap of honour with little Remy in my arms at the Liberty Stadium.

Dad taking Remy out for a bike ride at Center Parcs.

Mothers Day – I dressed Remy in a 'I love Mum' babygrow.

Proud father with daughter Remy.

Relaxing on holiday in Dubai.

Mummy and Remy watching nervously at Wembley.

Sharing a special moment in the players' lounge after the Wembley win.

My custom-made boots with my daughter's name on them.

A caricature of the three of us enjoying our holiday in Dubai.

Lazy Sunday with Remy.

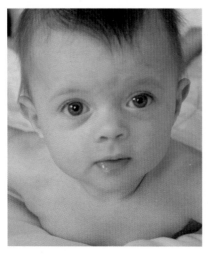

Two-month-old Remy.

Six months old.

Starting to walk.

Remy's first Christmas.

Cheese! – almost a year-old by now.

Lexy and Remy catching some sun.

Dad after the night shift!

My parents, Margaret and Alan.

With my dad at Sam Ricketts' wedding.

Dad laughing at my best man speech at my brother Stuart's wedding.

Lexy and Remy looking gorgeous in their dresses.

Three generations: my mum, my daughter and me.

Stuart, with his two best men: his son Cody and me.

With family and friends on Stuart and Natasha's wedding day.

Four days later, on the Tuesday night, Kris O'Leary and I were the only players to survive from the Friday night encounter. We beat Rushden and Diamonds in the Football League Trophy and I scored my first ever goal for Swansea City. Marc Goodfellow crossed from the right, I rose above the defence and scored with a glancing header. It sounds great, but I have to confess that I don't remember much about it. I'm just grateful to the Swans' website for that information.

On 6 December, after a 2–0 home win against Scunthorpe United, we were two points clear at the top. There then followed a terrible run in which we only managed one win in eleven games, a much needed 3–1 home success against MK Dons was welcomed; new boy Leon Knight scored a hat-trick. Perhaps the game which proved our inconsistency was the match against Huddersfield Town on 24 February. We were 2–0 up at half-time, playing extremely well with goals from Leon Britton and Lee Trundle. Then, we let the Terriers back into the game and they left the Liberty with a 2–2 draw. Our performance highlighted our lack of confidence as a team and the result meant that the visitors moved to second and we stayed out of the automatic promotion places in fourth. It was disappointing to throw away our lead as we had played in front of a crowd of 13,110 and the game was shown live on Sky television.

Given our unpredictability in the league, our performances in the Football League Trophy were a lot more consistent. In the Southern semi-final we played Walsall at home. Andy Robinson scored twice and, when he put us 2–1 ahead with just seven minutes left, we all thought we were on our way

49

to the Southern final. Unfortunately, in the 85th minute, they equalized. That meant that the game went into extra time, and with no further goals then on to a penalty shoot-out. With the penalty scores level at 4–4, Fox fired them into a 5–4 lead. It was my turn to take the next spot-kick. I have always fancied myself as a decent penalty taker, but I think if there is an attacking player in the team who'd like the chance, then they should have priority. I put my penalty attempt at the bottom right corner, and was happy and relieved to see it go in and put us level at 5–5. Graham Durkin took Walsall's next penalty and fired it over the bar. Tatey was next to go, and he converted the shot to take us to the regional final against Colchester United.

The Us were a strong side and leading League One at the time, with many of their players having experienced life in the Championship. In fact, a lot of them had played at an even higher level. They had Chris Iwelumo, the Scottish international up front, a big powerful player, someone I was going to have to mark in both games. At home, in a very difficult game, we beat them 1–0 through a goal in the 40th minute by Adebayo Akinfenwa. In the second leg at Layer Road, we went behind to a Neil Danns goal early in the first half. As a team we played brilliantly and, through goals from Leon Britton and Leon Knight, we beat them 2–1, and with an aggregate victory of 3–1 we were on our way to the final at the Millennium Stadium. Our opponents were to be Carlisle United, who defeated Macclesfield in the Northern final.

For the Football League Trophy final on 2 April, there were over 42,000 fans at the Millennium

Stadium. It was the first big final many of us had ever been involved in. Normally we would all stay in a hotel together the night before an away game from the Liberty but, of course, in this case, with the stadium being in Cardiff, security could have been an issue. Kenny felt that travelling down to a hotel on the outskirts of Cardiff on the morning of the game to have a pre-match meal and then on to the stadium would be the best option. As we left the hotel on our team bus and drove in, it was great to see that the Jack Army had taken over Cardiff city centre. The streets were a sea of black and white – not blue. Given the rivalry between us and Cardiff City FC, it was great to feel that we were playing in a home match. I believe that 30,000 of the gate came from Swansea, and they certainly made themselves heard before and during the match.

It was great to lead the boys out into that wall of noise in a cup final at a fantastic venue. I felt really privileged; I had captained the team in the previous and current season when Roberto Martinez was not playing, but I also felt slightly sad for Roberto, who had been the club captain. I knew that he was gutted not to be in the starting line-up. Roberto was technically a fabulous player, but unfortunately I don't think he was Kenny Jackett's type of footballer. Maybe there was a clash of personalities and footballing ideas but they never clashed verbally and, as players, we never saw them argue.

We won the final 2–1 with goals from Adebayo Akinfenwa and an amazing goal from Lee Trundle. His volley has to be one of, if not the best goal, ever scored at the Millennium Stadium. Andy Robinson played a long cross-field pass and Trunds hit the ball from a near impossible angle. The goal was every bit as brilliant as Marco Van Basten's famous goal for Holland in the 1988 European finals. Lee Trundle can be one of the best and can also be one of the most frustrating players to play with – all during the same game. The previous season, when we were promoted from League Two, I remember a game at the Vetch when Lee received the ball near the dugouts on the halfway line. Roberto had gone on a run through the middle of the pitch. We could all see that he was getting himself into a great position. Roberto was waving madly to show that he was clean through on the goalkeeper – if Lee turned and could just look up, he could play him a simple pass. Despite his arm movements and all the shouting, Trundle looked up and completely ignored him and shot from five yards inside the opposition's half. He missed by a million miles. Roberto was furious, and he wasn't too happy on the following Monday morning when Kenny called us all in to the meeting room to look back at the video of the game. When Kenny showed the incident all the boys were laughing as it looked so blatant on the video. but Roberto still didn't find it funny at all and sat there sour faced!

Having come into professional football late in life, I think Lee decided that he was going to enjoy every second. He was a showcase player – he had a great rapport with the Swans fans and wanted to show them how good he was. He was far too good for the defenders in Leagues One and Two but, if we were in a game where he lost the ball a lot or we were under pressure at the back, he became frustrating to play with, because he would never think of tracking back. Entertainers don't do that. But, looking back now, that frustration was worth it, because he helped us start what was to be a dramatic rise through the leagues. Roberto came on for the last few minutes of the final against Carlisle, so I went straight over to him at full-time and gave him the captain's arm band. We had always had a good relationship and, of course, it was the right thing to do, as Roberto was club captain and I was the vice-captain.

Once Roberto had received and lifted the trophy, he sought me out and gave it to me so that I could lift it in front of all our fans. That was a nice gesture, and I really respected what he did. It meant a lot to me and the rest of the players to win a trophy before the season had ended, and also to send the 30,000 travelling Jack Army home happy. (In fact it was our second trophy as, four nights earlier, we had beaten Wrexham 2–1 to win the Welsh Premier Cup at the Racecourse ground.) It was an even greater feat to be victorious on such a dreadful pitch. The Millennium Stadium playing surface has been criticized by a lot of footballers and managers. It's primarily used for rugby and concerts, all of which have clearly taken their toll on the pitch, and I have to say that on that day, it was one of the worst pitches I have ever played on. As we walked on to it before kick-off, you could see where the ground staff had tried to push the grass together. They had clearly not been successful, yet we managed to play some great football on it.

We were desperate to round off the season by winning automatic promotion into the Championship, as well as the two Cup victories.

Unfortunately, April was a bad month for us. We gained just one win out of six games, drawing two and losing the other three. After our home defeat to Rotherham on 17 April, we slipped into seventh place which meant that, with just three league games left, we were outside the play-off places.

I missed the next game at Oldham (a 1–1 draw) with a back injury, but returned for the home game against Southend. The Liberty was packed with 19,176 fans. Although Rory Fallon gave us the lead twice, Freddie Eastwood scored twice for the visitors and the draw was enough to take the Shrimpers into the Championship. We needed to beat Chesterfield away in our final game to make sure of our place in the play-offs. We hammered them 4–0. I remember the bus journey back to Swansea. After that game, many Nottingham Forest fans passed us on the motorway and made loads of rude gestures out of their windows because our win meant that they did not make it to the play-off spots. It made us laugh, which also made the trip even sweeter.

We faced Brentford in the two-legged play-off semi-finals, with the first leg at our Liberty Stadium. Their team included a certain Darren Pratley who would end up joining the Swans the following season. Brentford played very well that night and we did brilliantly to come away with a 1–1 draw to make it all to play for in the second leg at Griffin Park. We gave our best performance of the season in front of the Sky TV cameras. We were 2–0 up within the first 15 minutes, thanks to two great strikes from Leon Knight. We controlled the game from then onwards and, with late pressure coming from Brentford, we defended stoutly and got the fantastic win that our performance deserved. It's a game I still talk about with Tatey from time to time, mainly about how much we enjoyed the defensive battle and the satisfaction we got from that. The game gave us a 3–1 aggregate victory over the two legs, and a place at the Millennium Stadium for the final against Barnsley.

It was a wonderful feeling to drive to Cardiff for the second time within a month. It was also great to see the Jack Army take the city over once again. I bet Cardiff were sick of the sight of us! As a squad we felt that the Carlisle final had been a good dress rehearsal. We felt comfortable in the stadium and we knew the drill, the roll call and the warm-up times. The same applied to our routine of travelling to Cardiff on the day of the match, and staying at the same hotel before the game. During the pre-match meal, I looked around the players and felt, from the way everyone was talking and looking so relaxed, that this was going to be our day. We were all up for it, but I felt desperately upset for Roberto, as he was not in the squad. He didn't even bother to change. You could tell he was devastated and again, in his absence, I was immensely proud to be leading the team out in another final at this fantastic venue. This time the atmosphere had gone up a few notches, probably because of the importance of the game. It was great to win both of those cups, but this was a whole season's work coming down to 90 minutes and the prize of Championship football at stake.

The game started well for us. We looked sharp. Unfortunately, against the run of play we fell a goal behind. However, our heads did not go down and we got back into the game when Rory Fallon equalized with a tremendous overhead kick. I remember turning around on the halfway line as that goal went in, and looking up at all of our fans going crazy – it was a surreal moment for me, it just gave me goose bumps. We were playing great football and deserved to go 2–1 ahead with a goal from Andy Robinson. Unfortunately, they equalized, but we still felt we could win it within the 90 minutes. At the death, in added time, Tatey was sent clean through on their goal. This is it, I thought, we're through to the Championship. Unfortunately, he shot wide into the side netting, something I still remind him of to this very day. So, it was on to extra time. We dominated that 30 minutes but couldn't find the breakthrough. I remember looking over at Kevin Austin and it was only him and me in our half as Barnsley had every player back in their half defending for the majority of extra time. I was beginning to think were we going to make all this pressure count? Then, in the last minute, we had another golden opportunity to seal the victory. Trundle cut in across the edge of their box with the ball at his left foot. With Trunds in that position, bearing down on the goal, you would bet your house a million times on him scoring. He shot, and the ball went an inch wide of the post. Even at that stage I didn't think we had lost the momentum. So, it was to the dreaded penalty shoot-out. During the drinks break, Kenny was asking who wanted to take a penalty: there were a good few of us who wanted to take one. I was happy to if needed, but we had five players who were all confident. The last thing we said to each other in our huddle was to pick a place and stick to it. In those situations it's hard to know what to say – all you can do is try to focus the players and show unity.

During the penalty shoot-out the opposition took the coolest set of penalties I had ever seen. Bayo unfortunately missed his penalty which was our third spot-kick and it got to the point where Alan Tate had to score to keep us in touch. As he walked to the spot, I turned to Sam Ricketts and told him that the next penalty-taker was either him or me. We decided that it would be me, but in the end it didn't matter, as Tatey missed. All the penalties were being taken at the goal in front of thousands of Swans fans. It was sickening to see the Barnsley players run past us to the opposite goal to salute their fans. They were leaping up into the air and whooping with joy which was also really irritating. Of course, I can't blame them, as I would have done exactly the same. I went straight up to Tatey and told him that it took a lot of courage to step up and take a penalty, and that he should hold his head up high.

As we walked off the pitch I stopped and watched them lift the trophy. It felt horrible. I was devastated – we all were. It would have been easier to stomach if we had played badly, but we hadn't, we were the better team and deserved to win. But that's football sometimes, you don't always get the result that your performance deserves. I looked up into the stand, waved to my parents, family and friends who I felt I had let down; then I walked down the tunnel, only to be greeted by the FA drug testers who told me that my name had been picked, and I would have to undergo a random drugs test. 'Are you taking the piss or what?' I asked. 'I've just missed out on winning the most important game of my career, and you want me to come and sit in a little room, waiting for an hour to pee into a bottle?'

I was so upset about the game – my emotions were very raw. As I approached the door of the room, I think the whole enormity of what had just happened on the pitch hit me. I walked into the room for the test and I just burst into tears. I'm sure they must have thought, look at him, we've got a right one here; he must be as guilty as hell.

Leon Britton had been selected for the test as well, and we both felt even worse when we were joined by two of the Barnsley players who entered the room bouncing joyously.

After the test I went to join my family and the players in the players' lounge. To make matters worse, we had to share it with the Barnsley players who were obviously all smiles, enjoying the praise of their families and friends. In that situation there is nothing anyone can say to make you feel better. The disappointment stayed with me for many years and, even to this day, I can't watch that play-off video. When I was at Southampton I would often train for the whole week only to end up not involved for the matches. At Swansea it was different. I was a big part of the team. Every game meant something to me, and it was the first time that I had experienced such a loss. But those experiences spur you on to do better and strive for success.

During the following pre-season I trained as hard

as I could and was fitter than I had ever been before. I wanted to make amends and I was ready for the new season, feeling strong and good.

Chapter Four

AFTER MISSING OUT on the play-offs, we started the new season, 2006–7, confident that we could do well and hopefully make sure of promotion to the Championship this time around. Roberto left the club that summer, so Kenny called me into his office during our first couple of days of pre-season. He wanted me to take over as the official club captain. I was overjoyed, so proud, and instantly accepted. I was used to being captain as I had led the team out many times since my arrival, in Roberto's absence. But being club captain brought added responsibilities: I had to help organize community player appearances across Swansea, speak to the media on behalf of the boys, organize tickets for games, negotiate match and squad bonuses, go to the management to fight for what the boys wanted and also relay information to the squad which the management and club wanted in return. There were many different aspects, but it was something I enjoyed, and still do to this day.

Our first match was against Cheltenham Town, who had come up from League Two via the play-offs. We had a great crowd at the Liberty Stadium, with over 15,000 turning up for the start of the new season, as eager in anticipation as we were. Despite having a few chances in the first half, we struggled and by the hour mark we were trailing 0–2. Although we pulled one back through Leon Knight and the fact that we battered them for the last quarter of an hour after our goal, we still lost 1–2.

Three days later, when I led the team out for our next game at Scunthorpe, I had no idea that my second game was to be my last of the season. We got off to the worst possible start with Alan Tate being dismissed after 16 minutes. After about half an hour the match was still goalless, and I can remember turning to Izzy Iriekpen and saying, 'Come on let's dig in, we can get a result here.' As their next ball was played forward towards Scunthorpe's Andy Keogh and me, their midfielder miss-hit the pass, which caused Keogh and me to turn to chase the ball which had gone past us and, as I did so, the ground gave way beneath me. It's a movement all players do hundreds of times in a game, but unfortunately for me, because the turf gave way beneath me, all my body weight was on my left leg in a really awkward position. I felt a snapping feeling and the force on my leg sprang me back up and over on to my back. I knew it was serious. It was the first time in my career that I had suffered a serious injury. I had ruptured my anterior and lateral cruciate ligaments and also snapped my hamstring tendon completely away from its attachment area just behind the knee.

It took them a while to get me off the pitch. At first my overriding feeling was of shock and then it was soon followed by pain. I was in total agony and the medical staff gave me gas and air to try and ease the discomfort. I was taken to the hospital in

Scunthorpe and Kris O'Leary came with me. There was obviously a need for an X-ray. The nurse turned to me and said, 'Would you like to try to walk down to the scanning room?' I couldn't believe what I was hearing, and I often think that if I had been younger and dumber I might have obliged out of politeness. If I had done that, there is no doubt that I could have further damaged my injured leg and all because of walking down a hospital corridor. The X-ray showed no bone breaks, which was a relief at the time. The team bus came to pick me up from the hospital after the game; the coach journey back to Swansea I can only describe as the longest and most painful in all my life. My knee was so swollen and sore that I couldn't sleep. It became more and more painful the next day and by now the physios and I were really concerned.

The game was played on the Tuesday evening but, by the Thursday, I was taken to the BUPA hospital in Bristol where I was fortunate to meet Jonathan Webb, the former England rugby union player who was now a surgeon and specialized in knee injuries. He told me within one minute of looking at my knee that he wanted to get me straight in to the operating theatre. He was very concerned about my knee, and especially the nerve running down the leg, as he felt it could be trapped. Richard Evans, the Swans physiotherapist was with me also. I asked Mr Webb if he thought everything would turn out alright. He said, 'Garry, there seems to be a lot of damage. If you want me to be honest, then I have to tell you there is a chance your career could be over, but I won't know that until I get in and have a look.' I felt my eyes welling up. I think Evo and Mr Webb sensed this and left the room. This was the worst thing I could have heard. I burst into tears – was my career really going to end like this? My mind was racing.

When I woke up from the operation I was taken back to my private room. It was early evening and Evo was there but we both didn't know if the operation had gone well. Evo then had to leave for Swansea. I was kept in overnight. That was one of the most emotional nights of my life. I was high on the morphine in my system to help numb the pain and I had no idea if the operation was a success. I remember calling my parents and just crying my eyes out, not making any sense. My mum was extremely upset not to be able to be there with me. I think I rang nearly everyone in my phone book – I was struggling to control my emotions. I was asking the night staff continuously if they knew how my operation had gone, but of course none of them knew. It was a very long night.

Eventually, the next morning came, and around 11 a.m. Mr Webb came into the room and gave me the news I was craving: 'The operation went really well, I haven't repaired everything because there was too much to do, but the main thing was the nerve wasn't damaged.' Wow, what a relief! Mr Webb had released the pressure around the nerve and repaired the lateral cruciate ligament and had reattached my hamstring tendon. But, I wasn't in the clear just yet, as I had to return to the hospital in four weeks time to have my anterior cruciate ligament repaired.

In the days after the first operation I went back to Swansea and, for quite a while, I felt really unwell. I reacted very badly to the anaesthetic. There is a team photograph that was taken at that time and it still hangs at the Liberty Stadium today. I felt so weak that I had to prop myself between Izzy Iriekpen and Alan Tate. I looked worn out and more like a ghost than a modern-day footballer.

I knew that I would soon have to return to hospital for the next operation and have to go through it all over again, but I was determined to get through it and back into the first team. I have always had that kind of drive and determination. Players who don't do proper rehab will always pay the consequences sooner or later in their careers. I knew people were already writing me off, saying I couldn't come back from such a serious injury, but that just added to my hunger to prove them all wrong. As I tried to meet my own personal targets, the team had their own battles to contend with. For long stretches of the season they hovered near the top of the table. But, despite that, the expectations of the fans were incredibly high. In February, after three successive defeats, the decision was taken for Kenny Jackett and Swansea to part company – the fans had lost faith in him. Some fans felt he played a defensive long-ball game. I'm not sure that was the case. He never once told the players to kick it long. Bayo and Rory Fallon were the target men and Trundle played off them. As defenders we played to their strengths.

Sadly, Kenny never quite connected with the Jack Army. I don't think it was his fault; it was just the fans never really took to him totally – whether that was because of his style of play was debatable. They respected, but never loved each other. In Kenny's defence I have to say that he gave the team a winning mentality. He taught us to believe that we could win every game. Before he arrived at the Vetch, the club had been scrapping for years in the bottom divisions. Brian Flynn saved us and Kenny came in and built on what Flynn had achieved. He established discipline throughout the team and the club, and made us players into a solid outfit. Having worked at Queens Park Rangers and Watford he knew what was needed to turn things around. It is a tribute to the expectations he created that, in his first full season in charge, we won promotion to League One and the Welsh Cup. In his second season, the fans were disappointed that the Swans were not in the automatic promotion places. But he led us to win the Football League Trophy, plus the Welsh Cup and the play-off finals which we should have won. I think the Jack Army and the players should be pleased with what he achieved and the foundations he laid for the future success of the club.

Chairman Huw Jenkins called a meeting with the players. He told us that he had let Kenny go, and that Kenny had said to him that he felt some players weren't pulling their weight. Tatey's response was, 'Name names then chairman'. The chairman refused, so Tatey said it again, 'Go on, name names'. Over the years I have got to know Tatey really well, and we have become good friends. One thing about Alan is that he is not shy of saying exactly what he thinks. Sometimes you think why did you say that, but at other times you're happy that he does. The chairman again refused and went on to say that our assistant manager, Kevin Nugent, would be taking over for the next few games whilst the club searched for a replacement. Kevin Nugent was in charge for two games, the 2–2 draw away to Doncaster Rovers and the 0–2 home defeat by Scunthorpe United.

Before our next game, away to Yeovil, the rumours were rife about the identity of the new manager. During the pre-match meal, Kevin Nugent came into the hotel dining room and told us that he wanted to introduce someone to us. Officially we had no idea who was going to take charge after Kenny, although one or two of us had an inkling. In walked Roberto Martinez, our new gaffer and his first words were, 'Some of you know me and some of you don't.'

Those who did know him were probably thinking exactly the same as me. 'Oh, my God. This man knows so much about us. He has seen us at our best but also at our very worst.' As I sat there, I recalled our club trip to Magaluf in Spain. We went there to celebrate winning promotion at Bury. Roberto was of course a team member back then, and he came along on the holiday. This man, who was now my manager, had seen us all many times in the early hours of the morning in right old states, even having to put some of us to bed.

Although he didn't smoke or drink, he would always join us when we went out on the town. One evening we had gone to a nightclub in Magaluf. Holiday-makers had free entry and all of us went in ahead of him but then the bouncers stopped Roberto and refused to let him in. Because he was Spanish, they assumed he was one of the local boys trying to get in for nothing. Roberto was furious, and argued with them for ages before they finally believed that he was one of the team.

The appeal for Roberto at these nightclubs was that he loved dancing and being with the boys. The more he danced, the more he seemed to hit a natural high and would often stay until the very end. One evening the squad had gone out together but soon split up. I remember leaving him dancing in one of the nightclubs we had first gone into. Three hours later, at 5 a.m. in the morning, I returned to the first rendezvous and there he was – in the middle of the dance floor where we had left him earlier, still dancing. When I asked him where the rest of the boys were, he shrugged his shoulders and told me that he had no idea. I just laughed and joined him.

Just as it was different for those of us who had played with him, his new position must have been doubly difficult for him. Making that transition from former team mate to manager can't be easy and, as he stood in front of us in that hotel in Yeovil, I think we all knew that the relationship between us could never be the same again. It would be difficult to share jokes and practical pranks. Roberto claimed later that knowing us so well was a help. He knew how to get the best out of us. During the first couple of weeks the boys would occasionally call him Rob instead of boss or gaffer. Roberto wanted to nip this in the bud and one day called us all into a huddle on the training pitch. He told us he wanted to be known only as boss or gaffer from now on or we'd be fined. On breaking from the huddle Willy Gueret accidentally, and out of habit, shouted out 'OK Rob'. I had to laugh. Despite our initial worries we just got on with the job and the new manager.

At this moment in time I'm training to gain my

coaching badges. I'm already beginning to see that playing in a team and coaching a team is a totally different ball game. I don't think I was the only one to wonder how Roberto would cope under pressure – if the results went against him and the team. But when he came back to Swansea, he knew what he wanted to do and how to do it. There can't be many league clubs he could have gone to as a manager and received the instant support that he got at Swansea. Of course, as time was to prove, it worked both ways. He gave everything to the club and the fans gave everything back to him.

When Roberto Martinez became our manager he was to change our philosophy. The philosophy in the lower divisions was to mainly kick and rush, using physicality more than skill. When Roberto told us we needed to play to feet, I was ready; we all were ready for the new ideas. This was what I had been taught at Southampton. People now realize the importance of playing your way out of the bottom divisions. Brighton, Fulham and Norwich have all come up the divisions by playing good football. We are now familiar with the 'Barcelona style' and realize that what they do there is the pinnacle of football. This is what we all had to try and copy and we had to adapt. Because of the shift in football thinking and for what I feel is the good of the game, young players are being taught to develop their skills and with the increasing athleticism of players, moving the ball around quickly is becoming ever more important.

For that game against Yeovil Town at Huish Park, Roberto watched from the stands and saw his team go down 0–1. It dawned on me that I was still injured and out of contract at the end of the season. Although I knew Roberto well, he was now a manager and had to make managerial decisions. Thankfully, my fears were laid to rest as Roberto asked me into his office that week and told me that I was going to be his captain and not to worry about my injury and take as much time as I needed to get myself fit. He wanted me at the club and I was to be offered a new contract.

There were eleven games left to the end of the season and, of those eleven, the team won seven, drew three and lost only one. The final game was at home to Blackpool. Because of the great run the team had had, we were within touching distance of the last play-off place, but we needed to beat Blackpool (already promoted to the Championship) and hope that Oldham, who were also chasing that last spot, lost. At one stage we were leading 3–2 and Trundle had missed a penalty. Once Blackpool equalized, we had to go and chase the game and that left huge gaps at the back. The final score was 6–3 to Blackpool with Andy Morrell, the ex-Wrexham striker bagging four goals. Perhaps in the end it was just as well that the result didn't matter, because Oldham Athletic beat Chesterfield 1–0 to claim the last play-off place.

Despite missing out on promotion, I think after Roberto's brief time in charge there was a great expectancy among the fans and the players. It was interesting to see his new style and philosophy working out on the field and we were enjoying our training. He took the players from the British way of playing to a more continental approach. Having grown up in Spain and having played for Real Zaragoza, he was immersed in that type of play. In training sessions at British clubs players would normally touch the ball between one and two hundred times in practice. With Roberto, it increased to four to five hundred. He wanted us to have short, sharp possession and to move the ball around on the ground to feet more quickly.

All the training became far more structured and organized and he certainly brought continental flair to Swansea. He helped players to keep the ball and be more comfortable with it, instead of playing more direct balls downfield and hoping for the best. In addition to his training techniques, he built a good team around him, bringing in Graeme Jones as assistant manager. Roberto was passive in temperament, whereas Graeme had a little more bite. They balanced each other brilliantly and were an excellent combination.

Everything was changing for the better and my only frustration was that, apart from the opening two games, my whole season had been taken up with recovering from my injury. I chose not to take a holiday that summer. Instead I spent the whole of the break in my home town of Torquay training with my best mate Neil Aggert whom I have known since we were kids and were in the same youth team at Torquay United together. Neil was now a fitness coach and he would put me through my paces. I trained every day. I would check various internet sites during the break to see what the latest news coming out of the club was. I would read what the fans were saying and noted that some were writing me off, saying that I would struggle to play for Swansea in League One.

It made me more determined to break back into the team and be stronger and fitter than ever for the new season.

Chapter Five

AFTER JUST MISSING out on the play-offs the previous season, 2006–7 started with everyone at the club full of hope once again that we could achieve promotion. That feeling had become the norm now. Roberto's arrival towards the end of the previous season, and the work that he had done with the players had brought a real sense of expectation. But like every season, there were always comings and goings. Lee Trundle, a huge favourite with the fans, had decided to leave us and joined Championship side Bristol City. A lot was made of this move amongst fans, but Lee thought it was the correct decision for him at that time in his career. It was Championship football and, although we were confident we could gain promotion to that league that season, we couldn't guarantee it for Lee. And as I have mentioned earlier, he came into the professional game late, and this move was also a chance for him to earn considerably more money than here at Swansea. I, like everyone in the squad, was sad to see him go. I had become very good friends with Lee, and still am today.

I have to say Lee is probably the funniest lad I have met in football. He's quick-witted and always with an amusing story to tell. In fact, during pre-season in my first year at Swansea, the squad went away to Holland together and I was still getting to know the lads. At the end of a hard week, all the boys went out for a drink. We came back to the hotel late and Andy Robinson broke into the hotel's theatre. We all went in and sat and watched Lee do a 45-minute stand-up routine on the stage, all off the top of his head. He had us in stitches. This just typified Lee's character, always up for a laugh and good fun to be around.

We did have slight concerns over who would get us the goals in the future: Lee had been our talisman for the last few years and guaranteed us 20 goals a season. But Roberto made some good signings. One of them was Jason Scotland who had the hardest job of all, having to follow Trunds, practically filling his boots. Our first opponents of the season were Oldham Athletic, who had pipped us the previous season for the final play-off place. The game also marked the debuts of other summer signings such as Dorus de Vries and Ferrie Bodde, also the Spaniards Guillem Bauza and Ángel Rangel, with Andrea Orlandi to join us a little later to form the three amigos. The result didn't really do the boys justice. The game was at Boundary Park and whilst I didn't play, I saw the game. Trailing by one goal at half-time, the boys really felt that we could get a result. With over half of the game left, we equalized and for the rest of the match it was end-to-end with both keepers making some great saves.

I must admit that I hate losing at anything, especially football. When we lose, I take it very badly. Strangely, I didn't feel too badly about our defeat that day. I had seen enough to suggest we were going to be a good team and play some great football. There was the same positive response from the players and, whilst chatting to fans after that game, I realized that they weren't too desperate about the score and felt the same. I was back in the team for our first league game at the Liberty Stadium, against Nottingham Forest, which was always a massive game and a benchmark for us as a team. We earned a creditable 0–0 draw. Next we played Cheltenham Town away. At half-time we were losing 0–1 to a sloppy goal. Graeme Jones really lost his temper and laid into all of us. He was particularly mad with a few of us – one being me. During the game I had gone up for a high ball with their centre forward, and we both missed it. Graeme picked up on that incident and, staring at me he shouted, 'And you, you can't even win your bloody headers'. I was sitting down and Graeme was standing across the changing room. 'What are you talking about?' I said. The striker I was marking, Damian Spencer, was a big lump of a boy. 'Shut up, I can't win every ball, it's impossible.' Graeme moved towards me, I can remember thinking, 'If I stand up now and confront him, it's going to get physical.' While I was deliberating this, Andy Robinson, who was sat next to me, shouted at Graeme and told him to shut up. Roberto stepped in to try and calm things down – emotions were high. Eventually I turned to the rest of the team and said, 'Right we don't need to listen to this shit. Let's get out there and show them.' It's the only time I have ever argued with Graeme.

We went out and in that next 45 minutes we played some amazing football. With goals from Jason Scotland and Andy Robinson, we beat the home side

2–1 and the win moved us into fourth position. When Graeme was shouting at me in the dressing room, I felt that what he was saying was wrong. I suppose now, with hindsight, I think we probably all needed that kick up the backsides. We certainly proved ourselves with the performance. The fallout was all part and parcel of football. It happens sometime or another at every football club in the world.

As a team we certainly moved on.

Our next game was at Elland Road against Leeds United. Before the season kicked off, they had had 15 points deducted by the Football Association for operating outside strict rules concerning administration. That was a great impetus for us as a team, but it also inspired them. They were a big club and a real powerhouse in our division. The punishment had given them a siege mentality. It was them against the rest of the world.

We played in front of a crowd of nearly 30,000. At half-time the game was goalless and, as we chatted in the dressing room, we felt that we had done alright without being brilliant. In the second half they scored twice in five minutes, with goals from Jermaine Beckford and David Prutton giving them a 2–0 victory. Leeds had used the crowd to their benefit and, at the final whistle, we felt disappointed that we had missed the chance to prove ourselves against one of the top teams in the division.

The following Saturday we were at home to Brighton & Hove Albion. They were a dogged side, who very definitely came for a point, which they eventually got as we drew 0–0. As we left the field we were all amazed that the crowd booed us off. Although it was only a few hundred who were doing the booing, we might have understood if we had been thrashed, but we had gained a point against a difficult side.

The following Tuesday when we took to the field against Swindon Town, we still felt slightly aggrieved at the way the crowd had treated us after the Brighton game. It was a great end-to-end type of game against Swindon. Two good sides going for the victory. Both goalkeepers had made great saves. At half-time we were leading 1–0 through a Jason Scotland goal. In the second half Swindon equalized, but we scored a deserved winner through Warren Feeney.

At the end of the match we didn't acknowledge the fans. The players decided that if we won, we would all to get into a huddle before we left the pitch. Roberto didn't know that we had planned to do that. We were trying to show the fans that booed us that we would stick together, no matter what. After that game I do believe that those fans realized what we were trying to do. From then on we would always get into a huddle at the final whistle to show our unity, before going over to our loyal fans and acknowledging their support. I think the crowd took a while to get used to our new style of play under Roberto. They were trying to support a brand of football they hadn't been used to. It was also new to us as players, and I suppose you could say that we were all trying to adapt.

After Swindon, our next game was at Brisbane Road against Leyton Orient, who were flying high at the top of the table. At half-time we were 1–0 up and very few could have predicted what was going to happen in the next 45 minutes. After just twelve minutes of the second half, we were ahead 4–0 and towards the end of the game Warren Feeney scored another to make it 5–0. The other goals were scored by Paul Anderson and Darren Pratley, with two from Tom Butler. Just before this game I had started my own special style of celebration. I would wait for the players to get into a huddle and then I would jump on top of them. By the fourth goal I started to wonder whether it was such a good idea and began to think, 'Christ I could do myself an injury here if I'm not careful.' That victory sent out a warning to the rest of the division. The three points moved us into fourth place and this is when I thought, and we all thought, 'We can definitely be up at the promotion places or better at the end of the season.'

By the time we played Leeds at the end of December we had been on a fantastic run during which we won ten league matches, drew two and lost one, a 0–1 defeat at home to Huddersfield Town. The atmosphere at the ground was absolutely fantastic and, up to that point, it was the best we had ever enjoyed at the Liberty Stadium. A huge number of the Leeds fans had made the long journey and when we walked out on to the pitch, we could tell that the whole place was jumping. It also turned out to be a great game. Leeds had been on their own great run of form and, despite the 15 point deficit, they had got themselves to third place in the division. After just six minutes, Andy Robinson put us ahead with a piledriver of a free kick from 25 yards. Three minutes later, Jermaine Beckford who had scored at Elland Road, equalized for Leeds. After 23 minutes I went up for a corner kick. Paul Anderson had taken it and I rose above their defender, made good contact with the ball and managed to direct it into the net.

I must say it's the most important goal I have ever scored, because of the occasion, the importance of the game, and the team we were up against. Just 15 minutes later, with us still leading 2–1, we were reduced to ten men, as Ferrie Bodde was sent off for a late dangerous tackle. Strangely, this seemed to make the atmosphere go up another notch. Ferrie is a fantastically talented footballer, one of the best I have played with at Swansea. But he also has that little devil on his shoulder, which would sometimes get him into trouble, as proved the case here. Five minutes into added time at the end of the first half, Jason Scotland scored a fantastic individual goal, which meant that we went in at half-time, leading 3–1. It only took Leeds United two minutes into the second half to claw a goal back through Alan Thompson. Although we were a man short, we battled brilliantly and held on for a famous 3–2 victory. It was a great display and again showed the spirit we had as a team and, at the final whistle, it was fantastic to celebrate with our fans. The three points from the victory meant that we went five points clear at the top of League One.

We had hoped to match the success we enjoyed in the league with a good run in the FA Cup too. In the first two rounds we had comfortable wins over non-league Billericay (2–1 away) and Horsham (6–2; replay at home after a 1–1 draw). In the third round we were drawn at home against another non-league team, Havant and Waterlooville of the Blue Square

South League. Roberto rested me and I watched the game from the bench. It was one of those games we should really have put to bed. With 15 minutes left, the game was still goalless. Then Andy Robinson scored with a fantastic strike from 30 yards. A minute later their player, Brett Poate committed a scandalous two-legged lunge on Andrea Orlandi. A scuffle broke out and Tatey was sent off, while Kevin Austin picked up a yellow card. Three minutes from the end, Rocky Baptiste equalized, which meant that we would have to go to their ground for the replay. Before the replay the draw for the fourth round was made, and gave us the chance of a tie at Anfield against Liverpool, if we could get past Havant and Waterlooville first. The replay at their tiny ground was difficult. The pitch was almost waterlogged and lots of fouls and heavy tackles seemed to go unpunished.

In the first half we found ourselves trailing 0–3. On 38 minutes Bauza pulled one back for us and then, two minutes later, he was pulled down in the area and we were given a penalty. Unfortunately Leon Britton missed and so we went back to the dressing room 1–3 down.

It took us just three minutes in the second half to score through Jason Scotland and narrow the gap to just one goal. But we were unable to equalize and Tom Jordan, the son of Joe Jordan, scored their fourth goal and we lost 2–4. After the first game at the Liberty Stadium there had been a lot of bad blood between the two teams, mainly because of the tackle on Orlandi. They also apparently heard that Roberto had called them a pub team. A couple of their players whom I knew texted me before the replay, saying,

'Pub Team are we?' I think all of that bad publicity galvanised them, and they were definitely more up for the replay than we were.

After the final whistle, they were knocking on our dressing room doors shouting, 'Not bad for a pub team, are we? Well we've got Liverpool away.' In the replay I scored an own goal, but mercifully it's never been given in the football record books. They broke down their right wing and whipped the ball into the box. Their centre forward was just in front of me. We both dived for the same ball and it skimmed off the top of my head and went into the net. When I got up, to my surprise, the striker was wheeling away, celebrating the goal. As far as I was concerned he could have the goal, it was the only plus point of an absolutely dreadful night.

Ten days later, when we would have been playing Liverpool away if we had beaten Havant and Waterlooville, we had two games which would prove to be a pivotal part in our season. First we played Doncaster Rovers away; they were up there at the top of the table chasing us for promotion. On the bus to the game the radio was playing; it was saying that they were the Arsenal of League One and the best footballing team. We took that as an insult. This was perfect motivation. We gave another great performance and thrashed them 4–0. It eased some of the pain that we weren't playing in front of 40,000 fans and the TV cameras against Liverpool. It also helped that the victory took us eleven points clear at the top of League One. The next game was also away against Nottingham Forest, which was a ground we had struggled in the past to get points from. We gave an excellent performance again and came away with a 0–0 draw. Two powerful performances against our promotion rivals gave us great confidence.

Two weeks later we were away to Crewe Alexandra at Cresty Road. At half-time we were absolutely coasting, with a 2–0 lead. With ten minutes remaining, we conceded a goal, but were still confident of coming away with three points. Then, during added on time, Crewe scored and the game ended as a 2–2 draw.

As I have already said, if anyone lost their temper with the players, it would be Graeme Jones, the assistant manager. On this occasion, it was Roberto. He completely lost it and was so angry that he had a pop at everyone of us. I have never seen him so furious, and it was quite funny looking at Graeme Jones. He just stood there silently with a look on his face that seemed to say hang on a minute, that's supposed to be *my* job.

Once we left the dressing rooms and as we were boarding our bus, we could see that Roberto was still angry, so we agreed that we should all keep our heads down and not draw attention to ourselves.

As we drove back to Swansea, Alan Tate decided it would be good to put a DVD on for the whole bus to watch to help pass the time on the journey home. We all thought we would be watching a film, but it turned out to be an episode of the BBC series *Club Reps*. The very first scene showed a barman placing about 20 drinks on the counter. His opening line was, 'OK, who wants to get shit faced?' Given that Roberto is teetotal and hates players drinking, Tatey couldn't have picked something more inappropriate if he'd thought about it for weeks! Looking around the bus

I could see all of the players, including myself, were crying with laughter, quietly of course. I told Tatey to take it off, but he couldn't see any problem with the film. Eventually we got through to him and he turned it off.

As well as being a great player, Tatey can also make the team laugh sometimes without knowing it. When he first arrived at Swansea from Manchester United, he had never lived on his own before. I assume that his mother had done all his cooking as he wasn't much of a chef around the kitchen. He moved into his house and one day decided to cook a pizza bought from the supermarket. He saw the hobs on top of the cooker and, realising that they were roughly the same shape as what he was going to cook, assumed they were for cooking his pizza on. Turning on the hob, he placed the pizza on top, then went into the other room to watch TV. Eventually disturbed by the smell of smoke, he rushed into the kitchen to see his pizza basically cremated.

On another occasion he drove to a retail park. When he came out of the store, he put what he had bought into the boot and let himself into the car and sat in the passenger seat for a few minutes, before he remembered that he had driven himself and would have to get in the driver's seat if he was to stand any chance of getting home.

The other player who could make us laugh by doing or saying mad things was Paul Connor. It was a Friday night and we were playing away. Some of the team were sitting watching a match on television in the hotel bar. Paul came in during the game, looked at the screen which said that the score was 1–1, sat down and then looked at us all and said, 'This game has got 0–0 written all over it.'

Despite being so far ahead of other teams at the top of the table, during March and early April we had a slight wobble so that by the time we played Carlisle United away, we had won only two of our last eight games, drawing three and losing three.

When we played Carlisle United at Brunton Park on 8 April, they were in second place and five points behind us. It was vital that we didn't lose the game or else they would have closed the gap to just two points. Their manager, John Ward, was convinced that his team could still beat us for top spot and had said as much to the media. We knew what a crucial game it was and we played really well to gain a point in a goalless draw. At the end of the match we were celebrating with our fans. Jason Scotland saw John Ward and shouted at him, 'It's all over.' The manager replied, 'No it's not.' And in true pantomime style, Jason shouted back, 'Oh yes it is'. In the end, of course, Jason was proved right.

We went to the Priestland Stadium the following Saturday. We knew that a win against Gillingham would take the club into the second tier of English Football for the first time in 24 years. Fifteen hundred fans travelled down from Swansea, with another 1,700 watching the game on the screen at the Liberty Stadium. They must all have been disappointed in the 22nd minute when Dennis Oli put the Gills ahead. Just before half-time Guillem Bauza scored twice, which gave us a 2–1 lead which we managed to hold on to until the final whistle. The win meant that we were on our way to the Championship. I was very disappointed not to be playing because of injury, but met up with the players later and we partied into the early hours of the next morning. It was such a relief to have finally clinched promotion after some near misses, plus doing it of course with three games remaining.

When we went into our home game against Yeovil on 19 April, we were seven points clear of our nearest rivals, Carlisle United. We knew that a victory would make us champions. We lost the game 0–1, which was bit of a anticlimax. Although we battered them to the final whistle, we just couldn't get that equalising goal. When the whistle went, we all stood on the field slightly bemused. Were we the champions or not? We didn't know and neither did the fans. Then, the news came through that Carlisle United had lost at home to Southend United. So, being seven points clear with two games left, meant only one thing. No one could catch us, we were the champions of League One. Suddenly we could celebrate with our fans, although it was very strange not to have a trophy to parade around the stadium. The problem was that Leeds United had lodged an appeal against their 15 point deduction and the FA had still not announced their decision – something which still annoys me to this day. Quite frankly, it was disgraceful that we were denied our chance to parade the trophy in front of a packed Liberty Stadium. We had earned that right and it was cruelly taken away from us through no fault of our own. One of the fans had made a tinfoil cup with the words, 'Where is our cup?' written on it, which we paraded instead. It was now vitally important to us, as players, that we won our last two games of the season. Not for the reason of finishing on a high, but we wanted to make sure we finished 16 points ahead of Leeds United, so that there would be no disputing who was the best team in the league and the true champions. Winning the last two games would give us that.

The following Saturday we beat Leyton Orient 4–1 at the Liberty Stadium, but there was still no trophy. We had to wait until the following week for our silverware, when we beat Brighton & Hove Albion 1–0 at the Withdean Stadium. Furthermore, the FA found against Leeds United and so refused to award them the 15 points that had been deducted.

At the end of the game Brighton players, stewards and ball boys made a guard of honour for us to collect the Cup and our medals. It was great to have 900 members of the Jack Army cheering us on. I felt so proud to be captain of this team and was so happy when I lifted up the trophy. We had all come on such a journey of football education; as players, management, fans and as a club, we had all learnt so much.

On our way back to Swansea, we asked the coach driver to stop at an Asda store. I think Roberto was slightly bemused when he saw what was being brought onto the bus. I don't think, before or since, that there has ever been so much alcohol on a team coach. All the way home we wore our medals around our necks, drank and sang at the top of our voices.

Over the next couple of weeks I was thrilled to be voted Player of the Year by my team mates, having played some of the best football of my career – especially after the darkness of the previous season's injury, when I had seriously wondered if I would ever play again, along with some people who were writing me off because of this.

It was the icing on the cake for me and just showed that all the sacrifices and hard work I had put into my rehab was worth it. It was also great to lead the players on an open-top bus parade around the city, met by thousands of cheering fans. One of my favourite seasons had come to an end. Although, as I stood on that bus, I had no idea that there were even better times to come.

Chapter Six

As the 2008–9 season dawned, the prospect of playing in the Championship was fantastic. I knew I would be playing against teams and players who were not only top championship performers, but many with Premiership experience and pedigree. After the success of winning League One there was a great confidence around the club and there was a belief among many of the players that our style of play would suit the higher division. As this was the first time that the Swans had been in the second tier of football for 21 years, with many in the squad having their first experiences at this level, there was a sense that all of us, as players, management, fans and club were stepping into the unknown.

We spent two weeks of our pre-season training in Sweden and Spain, both fantastic trips. In Sweden we concentrated more on gaining our fitness. We spent the week training and running hard and were rewarded by Roberto with a team night out at the end of the week. Now when you have all been cooped up together for a long intense week, it's important to have this relaxation time, and it also helps new players integrate into the squad. One such new player was Ashley Williams who had joined us permanently from Stockport after a brief loan at the end of the previous season. We let our hair down with a few beers and had a good night out in the quiet town of Östersund. We had been given a 2 a.m. curfew, as we were leaving the hotel for the airport at 4 a.m. I can remember some of the lads sprinting up the street as Graeme Jones stood on the steps of the hotel shouting out a ten second countdown. Owain Tudur Jones and I had arrived about ten minutes before the curfew, and we were trying to hide our drunken faces from Roberto whilst eating the food that had been laid out for us by the hotel. So, with Owain and I at one end of the room, and Roberto at the other, all you could hear was this booming voice, 'Where's Monks? Where's Monks?' It was a very drunk Ashley Williams. There I was, trying to keep a low profile and this was the last thing I needed! Ash hadn't noticed Roberto and, as he got a bit further into the room, his face changed as Roberto asked him 'You OK Ash?' Roberto reminded him that we were leaving in five minutes and that we were to wear club tracksuit to travel. With this, Ash ran out the room to search for his bag which was somewhere in amongst the pile of bags in reception, but he only managed to trip over them, fall into the wall and set the fire alarm off, causing two fire engines to turn up at the hotel, therefore delaying our departure. I don't think Ash was quiet for the whole trip home, something which was extremely funny considering that he'd only just joined the club.

The week in Spain was geared towards gaining match fitness as Roberto had arranged games against four Spanish teams. Not only were they good games to play in, but they were also great learning experiences for the players. We were playing against teams who were playing similar formations to us and were probably a little bit further ahead of us in terms of progression of this particular style. So we took a lot from that week. The week ended with us playing a very young and talented Barcelona B team at their Mini Estadi (small stadium), a 15,000 seater training pitch in the shadow of the Nou Camp. We turned up at this magnificent facility and were lucky enough to watch the last 40 minutes of the Barcelona first-team squad training. Players such as Messi, Xavi, Iniesta, Eto'o, Henry, I could go on and on. It was a real privilege. For the game itself, Roberto had picked two teams to play one half each. I was in the first half team. What happened then is still talked about amongst those of us who are still here to remember the game. We were given a football lesson by a team of 16 to 18 year-olds. They tore us to shreds! It was so embarrassing. We came in at half time 3–0 down. Roberto was angry and embarrassed as well. The second half team went out and restored some pride by scoring three goals and earning a draw. But those of us who played in that first half say to each other every now and then, that no matter who we play, it won't ever get worse that that first half against Barcelona B.

So on to our first championship season in 21 years. Our opening match was away to Charlton Athletic. We all felt that it would be a good opening test for us. Charlton had a huge history and still carried the aura of a big club at this level, especially as they had only recently been relegated from the Premiership after a long stay at that level.

There had been a huge build-up in the press and amongst the fans for two weeks before the game. Wherever I went in the city, there were people who were keen to talk about the season ahead and especially this match. For many this occasion was a long time in coming as many years had been spent in the lower leagues with little sign of success. There was a great buzz around the club and the city and that was reflected in the 3,000 plus Jacks who made the trip to the Valley.

Going into the game I and all the other players felt so ready and were all looking forward to playing at this higher level. All of that excitement in the build-up and preparation soon turned to agony though. After just 60 seconds we were behind, as Charlton took the lead through a Mark Hudson goal. I could also feel the disappointment from our fans in the stands. What they and we had dreamed of for weeks was now in danger of turning into a nightmare.

We went in at half-time 1–0 down. As the second half progressed, from my perspective, the day was to get even worse. After picking up my first yellow card it was soon followed by a second and I was sent off with about 20 minutes left to play. Then, to compound my misery after my dismissal, they scored again to go into a 2–0 lead, which was the final score.

In the dressing room at the end of the match, the feeling among the players was that we had failed to play our usual free style. Perhaps we had let the occasion get to us. We had certainly been far too apprehensive in the way we played. Everyone felt down, but I felt even worse. The fact that the boys had had to play the last part of the game with only ten men made me feel terrible. In my whole career I have been dismissed five times, which I suppose is not a bad record. As a defender you always run the risk of picking up cards as you are always likely to make physical contact with the opposition as tackles, aerial duels, blocking and jostling for position take place regularly. Looking back on my dismissals from matches, I would say that only two were warranted. I believe that the others were harsh, as was the one at the Valley against Charlton in the season's opener.

Our first game in the Championship at the Liberty Stadium was against Nottingham Forest. They were many people's favourites to do well and compete for promotion in the Championship after gaining promotion from League One with Swansea. They had always given us a tough fixture when we played them in League One. Their keeper, Paul Smith, always seemed to have a blinder when he came up against us. Our matches against Forest were always hard-fought tight affairs, with two good sides going for it. This game was no exception. But we were determined to put the Charlton game behind us and get our season started. On the day we were just fantastic and played with real energy and style from the first whistle to the last. We won 3–1.

Our next game was away at Plymouth Argyle's Home Park. The game was televised on Sky Sports, and we came away with a 1–0 victory, thanks to a Jason Scotland goal. It was an important result for us. Not only did it give us back-to-back wins, but it also gave us the self-belief that we could compete at the higher level of the Championship.

Three days later we played at the Liberty Stadium in the second round of the League Cup. Having beaten Brentford in the first round we were drawn against Premiership opposition in the shape of Hull City. Apart from a friendly match against Fulham, this was the first competitive match at the Liberty against a team from the top tier. Our 2–1 victory against a team from a higher league gave us the real feeling that if we could compete and beat such a team, then not only were we going to survive in the Championship but also compete well in the top half of the division.

The reward for our victory was a home draw in the third round against our great rivals, Cardiff City. The two teams had not met for ten years. And apart from Kris O'Leary, not one of the current players had experienced this derby match between the Swans and their bitter enemies. During the build-up to the game Kris, our assistant manager Alan Curtis, and many of our fans filled us in on the background to this particular fixture, and we began to understand something of the intense rivalry that existed between the two teams, especially on a match day itself.

For weeks leading up to the game, there was huge coverage in both the national and local papers and also on TV and radio. One of the daily newspapers ran a poll amongst its readers to discover the most ferocious derby matches in the world. Whilst I expected the old-firm clash between Rangers and Celtic to be up there in the top five, I was excited to see that the Swansea v Cardiff game was in the top five as well. As a Southampton player I had experienced the animosity between the Saints and Portsmouth; also whilst on loan at Sheffield Wednesday, I was lucky to experience the steel city derby against Sheffield United and, to a lesser extent, the hatred between Torquay United and Exeter City. All were amazing atmospheres to experience, but nothing could have prepared me or any of the boys for what greeted us as I led the team out for our evening derby match in late September.

Swansea has always prided itself on being a family club but, as I looked around the stands that night, all I could see were grown men full of testosterone bubbling in anticipation. The match was being televised live on Sky and the atmosphere was absolutely electric. In the days leading up to the match, Jay Bothroyd, the Cardiff striker, had said that he wasn't too fussed about us as a team, and defender Roger Johnson had predicted a scoreline of 3–1 in favour of the Bluebirds, whilst Cardiff-born Joe Ledley had been claiming that he was going to put in a few tackles to make a statement, to let us know that he and the rest of his team were there. Listening to them giving their interviews, we all felt that there was an over arrogance about their team. We got the distinct impression that they didn't see us as equals, and that they were looking down their noses at us. They were all on high wages and it was as if they felt it would be easy to brush this newly-promoted side aside.

Being totally honest with you, my dislike for Cardiff has grown over the years. Whilst living in Swansea and feeling the passion of the Swans fans on a daily basis, you can't help but get caught up in the rivalry, and with the sometimes obviously biased Welsh media coverage in favour of Cardiff over the years, even when we were in the Championship together, it was frustrating. But my biggest dislike was the way certain Cardiff players carried themselves, although this attitude seems to have changed under the management of Malky Mackay, who has changed a lot of the playing staff. Michael Chopra was a prime example of the old squad: a good player but an absolute idiot of a guy. He would act all macho in front of his own fans but, in truth, he was a coward on the pitch, along with all the others who had too much to say for themselves and all thought they were better players than they actually were.

All of these remarks added fuel to our fire. In the first few minutes of the match Leon Britton turned past Joe Ledley and the Cardiff player responded by taking Leon's legs away with a wild swipe. He was instantly booked by referee Alan Wiley and, after that, we didn't see anything from Ledley for the rest of the game. He killed himself in that first tackle. I can remember saying to the referee, 'How dumb is that? He's been saying all week that he'd do that.' It made me wonder whether Alan Wiley had been reading Ledley's comments in the papers. It felt as if the referee had been waiting for him.

Apart from the first 15 minutes where we were a little nervous, I felt that we took control of the game. It was a great night, with good football played. It was goalless at half-time. Roberto told us to all stay calm and to keep doing what we were doing. During the second half we continued to control the game and, just before the hour mark, we were awarded a free kick just outside their box. Jordi Gómez stepped up and struck it, the wall jumped, Jordi kept it low and the ball skimmed the studs of one of the Cardiff defenders' boots on its way into the top corner of the net – the crowd went nuts. Our fans had been waiting ten years for that goal and the players celebrated it as wildly as the fans did. For the rest of the game we were in no real danger and we played it out to the end for a famous 1–0 victory. Our fans' celebrations at the end of the match were absolutely fantastic. Not only were we pleased to beat our great rivals in a derby match, but we were happy to win after all the negative things the Cardiff players had said about us before the game. Looking back on the game, they seemed to play as individuals, whereas we played as a team – that's what was key to our victory.

Just four days after that great victory and the fact that we had won the bragging rights over Cardiff, we suffered our heaviest defeat of the season at the Majedski Stadium, away to Reading. They hammered us 4–0 and that day we were taught a lesson, which I think we took on board. Under Roberto we had been encouraged to play from the back, but you have to be brave to do that and believe in your own ability. That day we learned that we were not as developed as a footballing unit as we thought we were. If you have adopted a passing game from the back you also have to, as players, manage the game as well. We needed to recognize when we could and could not play and, with us inviting pressure, we should have pushed up the pitch early on and let Dorus de Vries kick the ball longer to try and get a foothold in the game. That way we could have taken some of the sting out of the game and taken some of the pressure off. Against Reading, because we were trying to play football all the time, we were inviting pressure, and just couldn't get out of our half. An example of that was relayed by Roberto. He told us after the match that during the game we had got the ball up to Jason Scotland 14 times, but it had then been given away 13 times. That statistic showed just how much we had been boxed in our own half and were unable to break free, thereby contributing to our own downfall.

But we learnt a lot from that game and made up for the Reading mauling with a 2–0 victory at Deepdale away to Preston North End. That game will always be remembered for the wonder strike from Ferrie Bodde which put us ahead. I'm not sure how many yards away from the goal he was when he hit it, but I was the nearest man to him when he hit it, so I was first to celebrate with him. That shows you how far out he was. Deservedly, it won Goal of the Season as well.

Our next match was at home against Wolves, who were flying at the top of the Championship. This was a big test for us and a marker of how far we had come as a squad. We won 3–1 and, at the end of the game, we all felt that we had made a statement to ourselves as players and to the rest of the division. We realized that we were not the most consistent team in the league, but felt that on our day we could beat anyone.

Not surprisingly, our two games against my old

club Southampton stay in my mind. The first game was at the Liberty Stadium. I had invited two special ladies to the match, Carol Gogual and Julia Upson; both opened up their homes to me and they were great families to live with when I was a youngster coming through the ranks at Southampton. It was great to see them, although they are both stout Saints' fans! I never built up the rapport that I have with the Jack Army with the Saints' fans. I realized that the club meant more to me than I meant to them. Despite that fact, I still have a lot of friends in the city. The Saints were having a particularly difficult season in the Championship and looked as if they were heading for League One. We outplayed them and beat them 3–0. I was left with a strange feeling at the final whistle and, even during the game, I found it impossible to celebrate the goals. Perhaps my attitude came out of my respect for the two ladies sitting in the stands who had looked after me so well when I was in digs.

In the return fixture at St Mary's Stadium I had a poor game. During the days leading up to the game I was rushing around trying to sort out tickets for family and friends. Before kick-off I met several of the administrative and match-day staff who were still there from my time at the club. Again, I felt weird going back to a football ground which had been such a big influence on my early career. I think all the feelings got to me, and took my focus off the game. Early on I gave a weak back pass and the striker latched on to the ball. I ran back but struggled to retrieve the situation – I couldn't get the ball. They scored and took a 1–0 lead. Jordi Gómez hit a sweet strike and levelled the game at 1–1. We took better control in the second half without really being at our best, but the game finished as a 2–2 draw. It was an opportunity missed. Graeme Jones was very angry in the dressing room afterwards, but I didn't need him to tell me that I had had a poor game. I like to think that if I went back to St Mary's in the future, it would be very different and I would be totally focused.

Looking back on our first season in the Championship, I suppose you could call it the Year of the Cups. After victories over Premiership Hull City and our great rivals Cardiff City in the League Cup, they were followed by some impressive displays in the FA Cup. In the third round we were drawn away to Premiership side Portsmouth. As a team we were very good at assessing our progress, and Roberto always said that the best way to gauge our development was by how well we performed against Premiership teams, especially at intimidating places such as Fratton Park. The way we played that day was a measure of how far we had come as a team.

With 15 minutes remaining, we were 2–0 up. It was amazing to think that we were so in control of a game against a team that included several internationals such as Sol Campbell, Peter Crouch and David James. With so little time left, Pompey threw the kitchen sink at us. Every free kick or throw that went to them, they were pumping the ball into our penalty box. In addition to Crouch and Campbell, they had other tall players such as Nwankwo Kanu, Younes Kaboul, Sylvain Distin and Hermann Herriderson. Portsmouth were hoping that one of those players would latch on to one of those high balls. We were under immense pressure at that moment, and I remember looking around and all their players were between six foot three and six foot seven tall. Ashley Williams, Tatey and I were frantically trying to organize players around us. At that moment it was all one-way traffic – trying to tell players such as Joe Allen and Leon Britton to mark some of these giants was just laughable! I was marking Peter Crouch and I asked Joe Allen to take Herriderson and Leon to mark Kaboul. Despite all the pressure we were under, I looked around and couldn't help seeing the funny side of the situation. It felt as though we were in the land of the giants and were trying to fight them with two of the smallest players in the league. I remember looking at Ashley and saying, 'Just look at this, it can't be real.' For those last 15 minutes, we threw our bodies at the ball and managed to scramble the ball away, time and again. When the final whistle blew we had proved a point, not just to the rest of the Football League, but also to ourselves. After that game confidence was sky high; we had just beaten a team packed with Premiership and international experience on their own patch.

In the next round, we drew Fulham at home. Yet another team full of Premiership and international players. Again we gave a great performance. We were fantastic from start to finish. We were so unlucky to be going in at half-time 1–0 down. Unfortunately, their goal came from my own goal. They crossed into our area which was crowded with players. Dorus flapped at the cross and the ball came straight through the pack and hit me on the hip and went in. Despite my disappointment, we look back on that game with pride in our performance and realize that we totally outplayed them and did more than enough to win. I believe that this was the first time that our style of play reached national attention. At the end of the game Jason Scotland was interviewed on television and was asked if he was happy with our dominant performance. I think people outside Swansea thought that this performance was just a one-off. He told them he was not surprised in the slightest about our display and added, 'We play like this every week.'

In the league we were constantly within touching distance of a place in the play-offs. During November and December we set a club record by drawing eight games on the trot. During that run we weren't playing ugly and scrappy draws, we were actually playing some good football but just not taking our chances. The last draw in that sequence proved the point. At St Andrews, we drew 0–0 with Birmingham City who were chasing automatic promotion. We played them off the park and, at the end of the match, we were all agreed that it was a great mystery how we had failed to win.

During January and February we followed the draw sequence with an impressive run of results when we went eight games (including two Cup matches) without losing – winning six and drawing just two. With six games left in the season, we were still chasing one of those four play-off places. We had to play Cardiff away at Ninian Park. It was the last derby ever to be played at the old ground, as the Bluebirds were due to move to their new stadium for the start of the following season. It was vital for us to win this game, not just for the bragging rights, but also so that we could keep ourselves in the frame for promotion to the Premiership. The media had covered the fact that this would be the last battle between the two rivals at Ninian Park. As well as wanting to win, Cardiff City wanted the game to be a party. We were determined to spoil their party and, as we got off the bus, we realized what a massive game this was for the home team.

I followed Tatey off the bus. It's no secret that Alan Tate isn't the most popular Swans player as far as Cardiff fans are concerned. As I came down the coach steps, I could see grown men holding the hands of their children. The presence of youngsters didn't stop them, as the men frothed at the mouth. They hurled obscenities at us. It felt like if they could have got to the players, they could have killed us. Following the example of their parents, the children also started to shout obscenities. This has always amazed me. I have always thought that if I ever take a child to watch a game and that child behaved like that, I would be appalled and ashamed and wouldn't tolerate that kind of behaviour. What was happening in front of me just proved the bitterness that there was between the two clubs.

The animosity we had seen outside the stadium continued inside. I always warm up before a game with Tatey. He responded to some of the goading he was getting from the fans behind him by pointing to the Swansea badge on his jumper. This sent a section of Cardiff fans behind him crazy. It was quite clear to me that they would have happily ripped our heads off, given the chance. All this was adding to the tension and the atmosphere. Once the action started on the pitch, we took an early lead through a goal from Nathan Dyer. We played well and protected the lead and then, just before half-time, referee Mike Dean was struck by a coin. It was meant for Jordi Gómez, who had just been brought down by Michael Chopra in front of the popular Bank stand packed with Cardiff fans. This led to Dean awarding us a free kick. As Jordi sat on the floor, a Cardiff fan took aim with a coin; it missed Jordi and struck Mike Dean instead. The coin hit him on the forehead; I could see that the ref was feeling a little dizzy and disorientated after the impact. He started to double over and I grabbed him and tried to steady and support him. He certainly didn't look too good. Then, a few seconds later, blood poured out of his forehead where he had been hit. I waved to Richie Evans, our physiotherapist. He didn't know why I was waving at him, but eventually the message got through.

After all that unwanted excitement, we held the lead for the rest of the first half and went into the dressing room 1–0 ahead. Later I was asked by the press about the incident and I explained that the coin wasn't the only object being thrown during the game. Every time there was a throw-in or we were taking a goal-kick, you could see objects landing around the players. To prove the point even further, I spoke to a Swansea fan who was sporting a massive black eye later that night. He told me that he was in with the travelling Jack Army and had been hit by a coin that had been thrown. The Cardiff chairman at the time, Peter Ridsdale, said in the press that he was disappointed with my comments and believed them to be untrue. Bless you Mr Ridsdale, always trying to cover up the truth.

Just nine minutes into the second half, Cardiff City equalized through Michael Chopra. Both sides had chances to score but then, with just a couple of minutes of normal time remaining, Joe Allen, who had come on as a substitute, scored a fantastic goal. Scoring that late in the game, it was hard to see Cardiff getting any points out of it. I have a picture of me celebrating, and I have to admit that I look pretty happy. Then, just as we were thinking we were home and dry, Mike Dean made a shocking decision. He deemed that Ashley Williams had fouled Ross McCormack inside our penalty area. Ash had stood his ground as McCormack made a dramatic dive to the ground. The referee pointed to the penalty spot. I couldn't believe it – we all couldn't believe it. I think even the Cardiff players couldn't believe they had been given the penalty. It was one of the most horrendous penalty decisions I have witnessed. Had he allowed the atmosphere to get to him? Was he thinking I'll let them draw, then I can get out of here.

At the final whistle, I wanted an explanation from Mike Dean. As I, and a couple of other players were talking to him, Tom Butler, who had been a non-playing substitute throughout the game, ran on to the pitch to confront him, and shouted, 'Ref. Ref. You know that coin that hit you? Well it should have been a spear.' Tom was sent off by Dean.

In the dressing room, the atmosphere was terrible. We had known how much we needed to win and the draw felt like a loss. I'm sure if anyone had walked in and didn't know what had just occurred, they would swear that someone had died.

After that full-blooded derby match, we won three successive matches against Norwich at home (2–1), Barnsley away (3–1) plus a 1–0 victory at home against Bristol City. That victory put us just one point off the play-off places with two games remaining, an away game at Sheffield United and home to Blackpool. Unfortunately, we lost both 0–1 and finished in eighth position, just outside the play-off spots. Despite the disappointment of not making the top six, on reflection it had been another season in which we had made good progress. Given where we had come from in the last couple of years, we had proved that we were more than comfortable in this higher division, and could push for promotion.

With everything looking positive towards the start of the next Championship campaign, giving us another chance to aim for the Premiership, we were all hit by bombshell news: Roberto Martinez was leaving to manage Premier League side Wigan Athletic.

I have nothing but the greatest respect for what Roberto did for Swansea and the progress we had made together. Perhaps he felt the lure of Wigan, and the financial rewards that were offered, were incredibly strong and, of course, he would be reunited with Dave Whelan who had brought him to Britain in the first place. He knew the chairman well and he knew the fans well. From where he had started as a new manager with a League One side, this offer represented a great progression for him personally.

In a sense he had been lucky at Swansea because the players, many of whom had played with him, were very accepting of him. The chairman and board also gave him a free rein and he was able to take the club in the direction he wanted, which was a great show of trust from the club, as Roberto had no managerial experience whatsoever.

I suppose the problem for Roberto and the reason why many fans were so angry, was that, on his return to the club as manager, he had always preached about loyalty to the club. He had stated during the season, 'I was forced out of here as a player and they will have to force me out as a manager.' When Derby County expressed an interest in Ferrie Bodde, Roberto encouraged him to stay, telling him that the financial rewards would come if he stayed with Swansea and continued his football with us. Although he preached this loyalty, many felt as soon as there was a whiff of a move for him, he upped sticks and left. On TV and in the press, Roberto said that this was the hardest decision of his life, yet Dave Whelan gave a TV interview about the situation and claimed that Roberto had told him the move to Wigan had been the easiest of his life.

I think Roberto should have done more straight talking about his real feelings and then the fans would have taken the decision more easily. Instead of the direct approach, Roberto seemed to take the politician's approach, and he left fans confused and disappointed.

Then of course, after leaving he came back for Jason Scotland and Jordi Gómez. He also took his assistant, Graeme Jones, who had been responsible for about 90 per cent of the training schedule, goalkeeping coach Iñaki Bergara and Richie Evans, who had been club physiotherapist and fitness coach for eleven years. Despite all this, you still have to respect what he did for Swansea. He changed our football philosophy and gave us the platform to continue this philosophy. There aren't many people in any line of business who would turn down a job at a higher level which offered much greater financial gain.

Chapter Seven

WHEN I HEARD that Paulo Sousa was to be our manager, my initial response was, 'Wow, great'. He was a great player with a wealth of experience at the very top of the game. He had won back-to-back European Cups with both Juventus and Borrusia Dortmund. He had played with, and against, the highest calibre of player and my feeling was that if he could put some of that expertise into managing Swansea, then we were in for a great future.

When we got back from the close season, our first full week with him in charge was a bit bizarre: we spent it playing eleven versus eleven games, so that he could get a look at the whole squad. But this was strange as, going straight into games after a five to six-week break can be dangerous for players in terms of picking up injuries.

We travelled to Spain the following week, as this had been pre-arranged by the club and Roberto before his departure. On the first day of the trip we spent the morning doing a football session, but we hardly broke sweat. So, when we were told that we were back out on the training pitch that afternoon, we were expecting a hard, physical training session. Instead, we spent the whole afternoon practising defending and attacking set pieces. This was unheard of. Normally, that would come much later in the pre-season schedule. Pre-season training is all about individual players building up their fitness levels after the summer break. I also got the impression that week that Bruno Oliveira, the assistant coach, was not up to the task. Bruno had never played professionally, and while that hasn't stopped the likes of Arsène Wenger and José Mourinho from achieving great things, Bruno was not of that ilk. He had a Masters degree in Sports Science and Paulo met him when he was giving a lecture at a conference in Italy. As time passed, it became apparent that he was Paulo's confidante, rather than a top coach of a Championship side.

Even at this early stage, training sessions were very frustrating and often felt like a non-event. He didn't seem to understand the British idea that players must work up to a fitness level to build up for the rigours of the English football league. His approach was non-intensive. I remember asking him about his days at Juventus and what it was like training with all those superstar players and the sort of training he did. He told me that it was extremely hard, and they would often train three to four times a day in pre-season, which I don't think he enjoyed. I thought to myself, look what that training achieved though! So, for us to be doing the total opposite was extremely frustrating.

After Spain, it had been arranged by Paulo for us to go to Portugal for a week to continue our pre-season training. After the first day of training, Mark Gower and I felt at the end of the session that we hadn't been worked hard enough, not even broken sweat. When we got back to our hotel Mark and I sneaked out and worked on the treadmill in the gym. After that, we went for a run on the beach. We had to do this in secret all week because Paulo didn't like players doing extra training unless they had cleared it with him.

So the pre-season had come to an end. For me personally, that was the worst pre-season I had ever experienced and most of the boys were disappointed with it as well. Hopefully, I thought, with games coming thick and fast, training might change.

Timekeeping was a real difficulty for Paulo. He would often tell the players, 'There is a team meeting tomorrow morning at ten o'clock.' We would all be in on time, and there would be no sign of Paulo or Bruno. We would ask Alan Curtis and Colin Pascoe if they knew where they were, and they would tell us that they had no idea, nor had they heard from them. Then, at eleven o'clock or so, they would walk in. 'Oh yeah', Paulo would say, 'forgot all about that'. I don't know if it was all down to the Portuguese laid-back temperament, but whatever caused that kind of behaviour, it was a very bad example to be setting for discipline. Paulo seemed to trust no one and, as the season went on, it became obvious that only his opinion counted. In football you have to be adaptable to different personalities. Coming from his playing background, where he had been surrounded by great players, I think he found it difficult to cope with players who were not as good as he had been. His frustration would show and I think this affected certain players.

The longer Paulo was at the club, the more I saw the likes of Alan Curtis and Colin Pascoe becoming isolated from the management of the squad. He didn't trust the decisions of the medical team and, when they suggested a rehab programme, he would often disagree and devise his own plan. It was becoming more and more obvious that the unity we had built up under Roberto was disappearing.

As the club captain I have always tried to ensure unity amongst the squad and have a good relationship with the management. Yet at meal times after training, I would often see Paulo and Bruno sitting on separate tables away from the other staff. If they did sit with them, they would speak in Portuguese. He also preached a lot about how he believed that it was important that the squad and staff behaved like a family. Despite this belief he would do things that made players and staff feel isolated. I remember Paulo was keen for Kris O'Leary to leave the club. One day, in front of all the other players, Paulo said to him, 'Why are you talking to the club (board members)? Why will you not go?' Kris was a senior player, who had been at the club for twelve years, and deserved a bit more respect than that. It was incredible that Paulo didn't just pull him to one side for a quiet word, rather than try to humiliate him in front of the squad.

In our first match of the season we played Leicester City at the Walker Stadium. We had a fantastic first half and came in at half-time 1–0 in the lead. It was this game that showed us players that our pre-season training had not been adequate. We were nowhere near match fit and, in the second half, we had nothing left in the tank and lost the match 1–2. I remember that in the last 20 minutes we were all giving each other knowing looks. It was as if we knew this would happen.

Eight games into the new season and we had only won one game. A pattern seemed to emerge in all the games. We would start well and then we would have nothing left for the last quarter of the match. Because the training was not structured or rigorous enough, it was difficult for players to reach top fitness levels, and even more difficult for players who had been injured to get back into the team. They found it impossible to get to the fitness levels that are needed for a top game in the Championship. At the end of one training session, Darren Pratley and Marcus Painter joined me to do quick feet ladders and sprints. When Paulo discovered what we were doing, he shouted 'Garry! Garry! Come here!' from across the training pitches where he had taken a group of the players for a warm down stretch. We jogged over and Paulo shouted at me 'Who's the manager here?' I wanted to say, you tell me, I've not seen a real one all season, but instead I said 'You are.' 'That's right. Have I OKed this?' 'No, I thought I would take the initiative.' 'You sit down here and stretch like everyone else and respect the team.'

He always seemed to want to challenge me in front of the other team members. During a game against Crystal Palace at the Liberty Stadium, the referee turned in a nightmare performance. At the final whistle I went up to the referee and said, 'You've had an absolute shocker today. Next time you referee us, you owe us. You've had a stinker.' As I finished talking to him I was aware that I was being shoved in the back two or three times. I turned around and it was Paulo. He continued to push me in the chest.

'Why do you talk to him?' Paulo said. 'I wasn't being nice to him,' I said, 'I was just telling him he had a nightmare. I was doing your job for you.'

I was thinking to myself what the hell is he doing confronting me in the middle of the pitch in front of all our fans and the media. I didn't fancy rolling around fighting Paulo in the middle of the pitch, so I made my way to the tunnel. As I was walking towards the passageway, I could hear him shouting at me. I ignored him and kept on walking. I could hear him call again, 'Garry, Garry'. I just stuck my two fingers up in the air at him and kept walking. Once in the changing room, I was told that Paulo had got the players in a huddle on the pitch, and that he was shouting at me to come back to join the huddle. When everyone got to the dressing room, we were all silent.

'Do you not respect us?' Paulo asked me.

'What are you talking about?' I said.

'Do you not respect your team members?' he asked me.

'Ask them,' I said.

'Why do you talk with the referee when he not respect us?'

I decided to keep my mouth shut and not escalate the situation any further. I knew I had done nothing wrong, but there would be no reasoning with him.

The fans also grew frustrated with Paulo's coaching style. There was a feeling that we had gone from an attractive attacking team under Roberto to one that was playing too defensively. Despite all these difficulties there were, of course, some positives that Paulo brought to the club. In many games, his insistence on the importance of team shape served us well. In training he would stop the play and encourage the players to look at their positions and see where we were all positioned. That was definitely one of his strengths.

Although we benefited from his phenomenal knowledge of that strategy, there was a feeling that, when he sent us out to play, we were too defensive. Paulo's obsession with certain aspects of the game to the detriment of others was shown in his insistence that, as a team, we should change to zonal marking rather than man-to-man marking. We would have to attack the ball rather than worry about the opposition players. Because we had been used to man-to-man marking, it was important that we got our movements and the positioning right. This was something that served us well and, considering that we were not the biggest of teams, this was a clever ploy. The problem was that we would spend far too long on this in training – hours and hours practising. It wasn't long before it started to do my and the other players' heads in.

For our attacking set pieces Paulo decided to bring in an expert in this field called Gianni Vo. Well, at least we thought he was a set piece expert. It turned out he was a bank manager from Italy! When we had a corner, Gianni and Paulo encouraged us to make a run before the ball was to be delivered. We would start on the edge of the eighteen-yard box, and each make a run towards the opposition's goal, then back out to the penalty spot before making the same run again, only this time the ball would be coming in for us to attack. I suppose the idea was for us to draw the defender away from their goal. But this would rarely work. In the majority of games, teams got to know what we would do. As we made our first run in, then our run away from them, they just let us go as they knew we would be coming back! It clearly was not working but we were powerless as players to try anything different because Paulo would go crazy if you didn't follow what he and Gianni had designed.

On the day before a match, like many managers, Paulo would go through everything he tactically wanted us to do in the game. In the dressing room before his first game in charge, away to Leicester City, I was amazed when he started to go through everything he had said in the team meeting the day before. I sat there getting more and more anxious because, as team captain, I was supposed to hand in the team sheet to the referee one hour before kick-off. Paulo droned on and on. Thirty minutes passed, then 40, then 45 and still he was talking. I had to wait for him to finish before I could get up and head for the ref's changing room with Bruno. It meant that we were late handing in the team sheet and ending up with a very unimpressed referee along with his assistants. I told Bruno that I was unhappy. It was not professional to be late with the team sheets and it didn't stand us in good stead with the officials. For the first three games, Paulo continued to give these long talks before kick-off. In the end I asked Bruno to speak to Paulo to let us both go on time, even if he was still talking. There was nothing wrong with what Paulo was saying – it was just that all the players had heard exactly the same thing the day before. A lot of times the players were left to rush about to get changed and prepared for the game because of Paulo's ramblings. When I look back, my relationship with Paulo was certainly weird. But there were times when he was absolutely fascinating to talk to.

I see why he got the job. He would have interviewed well, and with his playing background the board probably thought he had really good contacts. The longer he stayed with us, the more I realized he didn't know many people or, more to the point, he didn't have the relationship with people to help him bring new players in. To be truthful, Paulo and Bruno didn't always know the names of players on the opposing team. Before the games, when we'd been given the opposition's team sheet, Bruno would come and ask, 'What position does this player play?' As players it's important to know as much as possible about your opponents, but it is even more crucial as management to know as much as possible so you can prepare the team. It was unbelievable that they didn't know where some of the opposition players played. I remember when Craig Beattie signed for the Swans, Paulo wasn't sure what position he played. How is that possible?

In spite of all the difficulties, towards the end of the season we were still in contention for a play-off place. Having played in some cracking derbies against Cardiff City, I was really disappointed that I didn't play in either game that season. During the home game in early November, I managed to pull my calf in the warm-up. The only good thing about that game, as far as I was concerned, was that we won 3–2. For the away game, on 3 April, I was out of the team injured, having picked it up at our 1–1 draw at home against Newcastle United on 13 February. During the week leading up to the Cardiff match, I had been training hard and was back in the squad. I was really convinced I was going to play because, in the team shape all week, it looked as though I was in the starting eleven. A lot of managers don't name the team until the day before, or some even on the day of the game, but with Paulo you could more or less have a good idea three to four days before because of the amount of team shape drills we did. Then, on the day of the game, Paulo pulled me over for a word, just before we got on the team bus to leave for the game. He said, 'I'm going with David Edgar'. Looking back, it was probably the right decision, but at the time I was gutted. I remember thinking but you need as many people as possible who understand this game. We played well and looked to be heading for a draw but a late Michael Chopra goal gave Cardiff a 2–1 victory.

Going into our last game of the season, we were one point behind Blackpool who occupied the last play-off spot. We needed to beat Doncaster Rovers at the Liberty Stadium and hope that Blackpool drew or lost at home to Bristol City. Lee Trundle, who had played for the Robins before returning to Swansea, had been on the phone to several of his mates at Ashton Gate. He told us that they all felt confident they would get a result at Bloomfield Road.

For the whole week leading up to that game I told

a few of the senior players that it was crucial that we were fully committed and focused on training and getting the result we needed. We would stress to the squad how important this week was. For the first training session of the week, Paulo and Bruno arrived late. They looked totally unprepared. For the first time in the history of the Swans, we had a chance of making the play-offs and possibly going on to clinch a place in the Premiership. During Wednesday's training, I was feeling really angry. As we were facing such an important game in a few days time, the training was not rigorous enough. During the drinks break halfway through training, Bruno was walking around all the players and asking what songs they were planning to sing on the karaoke at a team meal that Paulo had arranged for that evening. I was furious. I smashed my water bottle down on the floor. Seeing my face Bruno asked me, 'Are you not happy?' I said to him 'You're a joke. We've got the most important game the club has had in years this weekend. We're here to train not talk about what songs to sing on karaoke.' We went back to the training session. I could see Bruno was relaying what I had said to Paulo, and Paulo was just laughing, which infuriated me even more.

One story which summed Bruno up perfectly was when the Reserves were playing a game at Neath's Gnoll Stadium. At half-time in the dressing room, Alan Curtis was giving the boys a team talk on what he wanted for the second half, when in came Bruno. As Alan finished off his team talk, he looked over and asked Bruno if he had anything to add. Bruno replied 'Yes! Does anyone know where I can get a burger from?' Unbelievable – asked to give his input into the team, and all he could think of was his belly. Priceless.

So the game was finally here. Doncaster Rovers at the Liberty. We absolutely battered them but just couldn't find the net. Lee Trundle had a goal disallowed for a handball and Craig Beattie had a blatant appeal for a penalty turned down. Bristol City got a result at Bloomfield Road and held Blackpool to a 1–1 draw. That meant that had we beaten Doncaster we would have taken that final play-off place.

At the final whistle, I was beside myself – we all were. I couldn't hold back my emotions, I was so upset. I couldn't believe that we had missed out on this great chance of going into the play-offs and possibly up into the Premiership. Looking back now, I'm glad we didn't get into the play-offs with Paulo, as he did not deserve to be the one to take us to the Premiership. He had not earned that right.

Paulo certainly didn't put the work in and our experiences throughout the season certainly proved that point. Under most other coaches and managers, training is structured and planned to get the maximum out of players whilst keeping them excited and enthused for training everyday. That was never the case with Bruno and Paulo and, as I've already said, I would often work out my own training regime. It was such a strain to go from working hard every day under Roberto to doing virtually nothing. It was the attitude of the boys in the squad and our team togetherness that got us so close to the play-offs. If we had had a different squad, full of players who were not so self-motivated, then I think we would have had an awful season. In terms of the progression Swansea City had made under Kenny Jackett and then Roberto, I saw Paulo's time in charge as a wasted season. Yes, we finished seventh, which was one place higher than the previous season, but I put that achievement down to the attitude of the players rather than anything Paulo Sousa gave us.

At the end of the 2010–11 season, it was the first time in my football career that I began to think that I couldn't go through another season like this. Then of course Leicester City came looking for Paulo. Looking back, my impression is that the board had been looking to off-load him for quite a while. For some time the chairman had been coming down to watch every training session, which is very unusual. In the end, the board must have felt that Christmas had come early. Instead of thinking of how much they would have to pay Paulo off if they sacked him, they were suddenly receiving compensation for him. There was no fight to keep him and Paulo was on his way. So, for the second successive season, we were to start the following season without a manager.

Once Paulo arrived at the Walker Stadium, their captain, Matt Oakley, whom I had known since my days at Southampton, telephoned me to ask about Paulo. I'm not one to go around bad-mouthing people, so I told Matt to make his own mind up and ring me back in two months time and tell me what he thought. After two weeks Matt was on the phone again.

'Who the hell is this bloke?'

I don't believe it's a coincidence that Paulo didn't last long in that job either.

Chapter Eight

BEFORE THE START of the 2010–11 season and while Paulo was still our manager, I received a phone call from Jackie Rockey, the club secretary. She told me the devastating news that one of our players, Besian Idrizaj, had died at his home in Austria. At that stage, news was just filtering through and no one at the club had all the details, but it appeared that he had died of a heart attack. Shefki Kuqi, who was very close to Besian, flew out to Austria to comfort the family.

The whole situation was horrible and shocking. You just don't expect to hear news like that, especially about a team mate who was only twenty-two. Everyone at the club was stunned. When he first joined us, we were all aware that he had had health problems in the past, but we had also watched him getting better and better, fitter and fitter. Just a few days before the end of the season I had a long talk with Besian. From watching him in training, I knew that he had talent and from talking to him I could see that he was determined to take it as far as he could. I told him that he was looking stronger and fitter than in the past and encouraged him to come back for the next pre-season and have a real go at getting a first-team spot. He said he was determined and looking forward to doing just that. Seven days later he was dead and I, along with all the players and staff and the club as a whole, had to come to terms with the fact that we would never see him again.

Every day the fans laid wreaths and messages of condolence at the stadium. With the players who were still left in Swansea and with some members of the administrative staff, I arranged a memorial service which we held outside the gates of the stadium. The short service was taken by Kevin Johns, the club chaplain. It was the least we could do to pay our respects to Besian and his family. We were very fortunate to have Shefki Kuqi, who'd spent a lot of time in Austria with Besi's family and friends. I arranged that he took flowers on behalf of the team members and staff to the funeral service. It's at times like this that you put things in perspective. Nothing compares to the loss of a loved one or close friend or, as in this case, a team mate. Because we had been such a tight-knit group, it really hit us hard and we felt as though we had lost a brother. And still, to this very day, Besian is never far away from our thoughts.

Missing out on the play-offs and then the news of Besian's death made it a dark summer. Then, of course, Paulo left for Leicester. This meant that, as well as the heavy cloud hanging over the club because of Besian's death, there was now an added uncertainty of what the future held. When a club is looking for a new manager, players grow unsure whether they will be staying at the club. For two weeks after Paulo left, we were in a state of limbo. But it was important that the club made the right appointment. Although

Colin Pascoe and Alan Curtis trained us hard and did a great job of steadying the ship in this period, it was inevitable that in such circumstances there would not be the same sense of intensity for the players. They were aware that they would have to start from scratch when the new man came to take control.

Rumours flew around the Liberty Stadium and in the press, linking people such as Gareth Southgate and Garry Speed with the vacancy. In the end the board plumped for Brendan Rodgers, who had managed Watford and Reading and had also been a coach at various levels with Chelsea. As a club, we certainly hit the jackpot with this appointment. They couldn't have found a better manager or a better person. After the previous season and Besian's death, Brendan Rodgers was exactly what we needed.

From day one Brendan lifted the place and the team. He took us back to the type of training that we were used to and had missed so badly. We believed in him as a man and believed in his vision. He wanted us to play in an attacking way and he had the players at the club who could do that for him. In addition, from his time at Chelsea, where he had coached under José Mourinho, he had excellent contacts. There was a real sense amongst the squad that we were now heading in the right direction and looking forward to working under the management of Brendan.

After all the upheaval in the close season, it has to be said that preparations for the pre-season tour of Holland were not the best. Our first two games were total non-contests. We beat third tier side W Haglandia 4–1 and then, in the next game, we played non-league VCS whom we demolished 9–1. It was only in our final game against the top Dutch side Den Haag that we were stretched. We lost the game 0–1 which was also the score at half-time. During the dressing room break, the new manager pointed out that we needed to forget about last season and become more attacking – unleash the shackles, I guess. He realized that because we had been so defensive in the previous season it was still very much our mindset. Of course, deciding that you need to be more of an attacking force is easier said than done, but we did play much better in the second half and put our hosts under a lot more pressure. The gaffer also realized that a lot of work was needed to change us from an overly defensive outfit to a team that attacked freely. Despite feeling that we could have benefited from some tougher challenges in our first two matches in Holland, by the time our pre-season came to an end the feeling in the camp was that we were pretty much where we wanted to be in terms of personal fitness and appetite for the new term.

After the disappointment of losing our first game 0–2 away to Hull City, we played our first Championship home game under Brendan against Preston North End. This match marked the debut of a young player called Scott Sinclair. Because of Brendan's connections, he was able to sign him from Chelsea. This was a real coup for the club. Scott was a fantastic addition to the squad, and with Scott on one wing and Nathan Dyer on the other, we terrorized Preston and beat them 4–0. The game was also dedicated to the memory of Besian. The players, staff and fans showed their unity before kick-off by taking part in a minute's silence; one whole side of the stadium held up cards and scarves that read the number 40, Besian's squad number. Funnily enough the scoreline matched his squad number. A perfect tribute.

Very early on, Brendan had an opportunity to return to two of his former clubs. On 28 September we went to Vicarage Road to take on Watford. It was vital that we should win this one, not just for Brendan but because of our disappointing away form up to that point. We had won our four home games, but had lost on the road to Hull City, Norwich, Leeds and Nottingham Forest. The strange thing was that in all our defeats we had not played particularly badly, but we were desperate to pick up our first three points away from home. Scott Sinclair, Stephen Dobbie and Frank Nouble put us 3–0 ahead, but then, with just a few minutes remaining, Watford staged a fantastic comeback. Martin Taylor and Troy Deeney scored to bring them within one goal of us and then, right at the death, Martin Taylor headed home. Mercifully, the linesman flagged and the goal was disallowed for offside. We came away with a 3–2 victory. Looking back there are always four or five key games in a season and this was definitely one of those. As well as getting the monkey off our back and recording our first away win, it was also a big boost and a platform to push on with our season.

Eleven days later, following a goalless draw at home to Derby County, we visited the other team Brendan had managed. At the Madjeski Stadium another goal from Scott Sinclair, his ninth in ten games, gave us a 1–0 victory over Reading (although Nathan Dyer hit the bar and Stephen Dobbie and Andrea Orlandi came close to scoring). Even though Reading came on strongly at the end, we defended well and earned a well-deserved victory. All the players were happy and so pleased for the gaffer that we had won at both his old clubs. Although he would never say such a thing, I'm sure he must have been smiling inwardly and must have felt vindicated.

Towards the end of October, we were drawn away against Wigan Athletic in the League Cup. This was a huge game for the fans as it was the first time that the Swans had played against Roberto since he left the Liberty. A game like this can often put the manager in a difficult position. Of course, the target is always to try to progress as far as possible in cup competitions, but it's also a chance for the manager to rest a few players and give some of the other members of the squad a run out. But this particular game, because of the history between Roberto and Swansea and the fact that so many travelling Jacks were there, made those decisions even harder. But what you have to remember is the bigger picture. It was a perfect chance to change the team and that's what the manager did. Although I was on the bench, I ended up playing for most of the game as I replaced Albert Serran who got injured after 19 minutes. We played well and didn't deserve to lose 0–2. I was gutted at the final whistle, partly because it would have been wonderful to beat our ex-manager's side, but I was also disappointed for the fans. Four thousand, five hundred members of the Jack Army had made the long journey from Swansea to the north-west of England. They were a huge presence in a crowd of just over 11,000. Despite the defeat it didn't really affect our season and we continued to do well in the league.

Two weeks later it was time for another Welsh derby, away to Cardiff City. I was pleased to return from a one-match suspension and captain the team. Yet again there was an electric atmosphere and the stadium was packed. Prior to the game, the Armed Forces were paraded in front of the fans. As we came in from our warm-up there were around 20 to 30 of them in the tunnel. Quite intimidating, seeing we had to walk right through them and I was thinking they were bound to be Cardiff fans, but it turned out that most were actually Swansea fans, as they were chanting our names. They seemed as up for the game as we did! We dominated the match from beginning to end and, with 15 minutes to go, Martin Emnes, who was on loan from Middlesbrough, scored the only goal of the game. It was great to go on to the enemy's patch and turn them over, especially as the match was live on BBC television. The result sent a message out to the rest of the league and also to the many pundits and critics that had Cardiff down as favourites out of the two teams for promotion. The only disappointment was that they managed to beat us in the return fixture at the Liberty through a great strike by Craig Bellamy.

With five games to go to the end of the season, we were still within touching distance of the automatic promotion spots but, after a 1–2 loss away to Burnley, it meant that we slipped to five points behind the last automatic promotion spot. After a goalless draw at Fratton Park against Portsmouth, we secured a play-off place two days later with a 4–1 home victory over Ipswich Town at the Liberty Stadium. That alone was a massive achievement and what the players and Brendan had achieved on the pitch in his first season in charge was amazing. He brought professionalism to the club. He pushed us to our limits and we pushed ourselves for him every day. We were prepared to do that for him, as we bought into his vision and respected him. We were all convinced that it was not our fault that we had failed to get into the play-offs the season before. Now we had made it with arguably the best manager the club had ever had. The gaffer had honed his skills in coaching and the management of players since his early 20s, and that expertise came across in his training sessions and games. Everything he presented to us was easy to buy into, and mentally, physically and tactically he took us to a level that no other manager before had been able to take us.

The last two games of our season were against Millwall away and Sheffield United at home. I was in the starting line-up for the game at the New Den, but I was struggling against a stomach bug and sickness. I had barely slept the night before. I told our physiotherapist, Kate Rees, who relayed the news to the gaffer that I wasn't feeling brilliant. So I was rested. We won the game 2–0 with an impressive performance.

Our final league game of the season was at home to Sheffield United. I was dropped to the bench. Manager Brendan Rodgers called me into his office the day before to tell me he was going with the same starting eleven that had played against Millwall the previous week. I wasn't happy as I had been playing

Owain Tudur Jones, Sam Ricketts and me after winning the Football League Trophy, 2005/06.

With the Football League Trophy, 2006.

Finally getting my hands on the League One Trophy.

The fans' tribute to Besian Idrizaj at the Liberty Stadium.

Introducing the team at the Millennium Stadium for the Football League Trophy.

Rising above Manchester Utd's Patrice Evra.

Battling for the ball with Manchester Utd striker Javier Hernández.

With my old team mate Darren Pratley in the FA Cup match at Bolton.

The look of despair after losing out on the final play-off place by a point, after drawing at Doncaster.

Heading for the tunnel after being sent off in our first Championship league game away to Charlton, 2008/09.

With referee Mike Dean after he was struck by a coin on the forehead during the last ever Cardiff vs Swansea match at Ninian Park. Feeling dizzy, ref?

Me (signed on a free) and Chelsea striker Fernando Torres (signed for just the £50 million).

Moaning, as usual, at the referee's assistant!

A rare sight – me scoring a goal againt Leeds Utd at the Liberty Stadium.

Doing the Alan Shearer celebration with a one-arm raise.

In action in one of the many south Wales derbies.

Trying to get the ball off Manchester Utd's Ryan Giggs – not an easy thing to do.

My first season as a Swan at the Vetch, 2004.

Saluting the travelling Swansea fans after a famous victory over bitter rivals Cardiff.

Party time after winning League One.

With the boys, killing time on a pre-season tour to Holland. Shefki Kuqi looks happy!

Defenders shouldn't really wear gloves. (But it was cold!)

In action against Spurs at the Liberty Stadium.

Me against the £35 million Andy Carroll at Anfield.

A great feeling at the final whistle after a victory against Cardiff.

Clapping the Swansea fans at the last ever Cardiff vs Swansea derby at Ninian Park.

Ashley Williams, Mark Gower and me at a Swansea awards dinner.

With the boys at one of our many community presentations.

With Lee Trundle at a fans' forum.

Me and Tatey having a go on the karaoke at a club party.

The Swans boys in fancy dress during one of our Christmas parties.

Me and Alan Tate as Mario and Luigi – can you guess who's who?!

Driving Leon Brittan around in his booster seat.

With my good mate Sam Ricketts on a holiday in Dubai.

Leading the team out at Wembley with Brendan Rodgers, the boss.

Lifting the Cup at Wembley – a dream come true.

Party time!

Still party time!

We did it! Alan Tate, me and Leon Brittan – from League Two to the Premiership, all together.

Soaking up the party atmosphere.

One of my proudest moments – looking up at all the happy faces of the Jack Army at Wembley.

Me and Tatey kicking off the dressing room celebrations at Wembley. Champagne can really sting the eyes!

Now the eyes are burning!

With my room mate Mark Gower and the trophy.

Open-top bus parade after clinching promotion to the Premiership.

Look what I found in the Cup – my little Remy!

Me and Ashley Williams with the Cup at the post-Wembley party. (I think Ash thought it was going to be sunny inside Morgans hotel.)

On stage at the Rod Stewart concert. We make a good boy band!

More celebrating through the streets of Swansea.

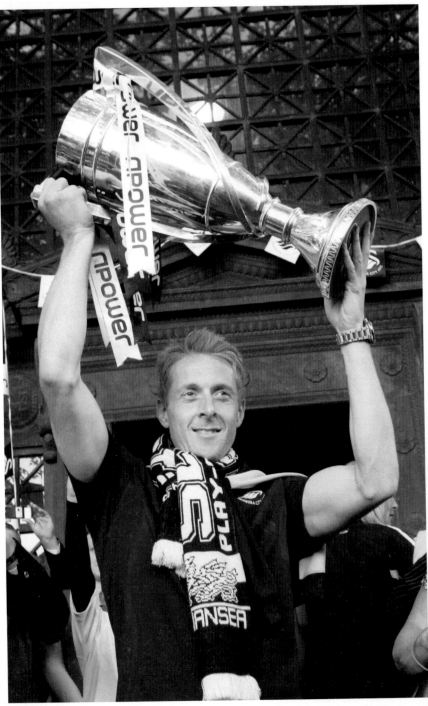

Lifting the Cup outside Swansea Town Hall in front of tens of thousands of supporters.

regularly before this. Also, with the play-off games so close, I knew that the chance of me starting in those games and leading the team out was now highly unlikely, which was a horrendous thought to contend with. I'd been through so much with the club over the years and didn't want to miss out on these special occasions. We swept aside a young Sheffield Utd team 4–0. I was brought on as sub for the last 20 minutes. It's a tradition to do a lap of honour after the last home league game of each season, to show your appreciation to the fans for their support.

Only this time, it was extra special for me and my fiancée, Lexy, as we had just become first-time parents. So I was able to take my daughter Remy, who was only three months old at the time, on the lap of honour with me. A lot of the squad had become parents that year as well, and did the same thing. As I led the squad on the walk, after a quarter of a lap I remember looking back at my team mates and thinking, wow, I've never seen so many babies! We looked like a group of nursery workers out on a day trip. Great memories! We had finished in third place in the league, meaning that we had drawn Nottingham Forest in the play-off semi-finals. The first leg was a 7.45 p.m. kick-off on Thursday, 12 May at the City Ground. During the week leading up to the game, all I could think about was if I was going to be starting the game or not. We travelled up on the Wednesday. I roomed with Mark Gower and when we both discovered that neither of us was in the starting line-up, our hotel room became a very unhappy place. We were both on the bench. I have nothing but the greatest respect for Brendan. He has been brilliant with me from the day he became manager and I think he is a great person as well as a top manager, the best I have worked with. Part of me was feeling let down, because I was thinking, I have been here all these years and I have played most of the games this season. I suppose if it had been another manager, I would have thrown my toys out of the pram, but Brendan is so open and honest with the players that you can't react negatively.

I also know that, as the club captain, it was vitally important that I didn't show any annoyance or frustration around the other players. It was vital that they stayed focused on the job in hand. During the warm-up our players were in a great mood. Despite our positive feelings, we all knew that we probably faced the hardest route to the Wembley final. Forest were definitely the form team, putting together a brilliant run towards the end of the season.

I have never experienced anything quite as intense as the media build up to the play-offs. Everyone mentioned the fact that, failure at this point, could lose the club £90 million and this only intensified the hype. I also feared that if we failed to reach the Premiership it would dismantle the side. We would lose our best players to bigger clubs and, for older players like myself, it marked possibly the last chance of getting to the Premiership and playing at the highest level.

The atmosphere was great. A full house, buoyed with 4,000 plus travelling Jacks who were determined to make themselves heard. The match kicked off and I settled myself on the bench to watch. Only I didn't stay sitting there for too long. Barely a couple of minutes into the game, as I bent down to put my shirt and shin pads on the floor, I could hear the crowd roaring as if they had scored a goal. I turned around and saw both teams surrounding the referee, aware that something had happened. Neil Taylor had gone into a tackle with his leg raised. Next thing I knew Neil was being sent off. Those who saw it felt that Mike Dean's decision was harsh and that there was no real intent in his tackle. Dean had made a few strange decisions against us over recent seasons, so to many I guess it was no surprise. I was told by the gaffer to go and warm up. I was still a bit bemused by what had just happened – I think we all were. As I warmed up, I was half looking at the manager to see what he was going to do. After about a minute of warming up, the gaffer called me over and asked if I was ready. I was. I was going to have to play to keep four of us in defence, sacrificing Stephen Dobbie instead up front. I remember talking to Mark Gower in our hotel room the previous night. I was telling him that nearly every time I'd been on the bench something would happen where I would have to come on. It happened in the Carling Cup match against Wigan, where I was sent on after just 15 minutes. And it was happening now. Having spent the last 24 hours thinking that I was going to miss out on this massive occasion, I would end up playing for almost the entire 90 minutes.

As I hadn't imagined playing for so long, I was up against it right from the start. Not trying to sound a hero, but I was just getting over a virus I had caught earlier that week. I had been sick for a couple of days and had lost weight. On top of that I also had a back spasm at the start of the week.

That night I was proud to be a part of what I believe was the best performance by a Swansea team since I joined the club. Despite being down to ten men, we dominated the rest of the first half. I don't think Billy Davies could quite believe it. I have seen that look so many times from opposition managers over the years – not really knowing what to do to counteract our play. After the break it was a different game. We were up against a determined Forest as they poured forward in an attempt to take a win into the next leg. Despite their non-stop pressure, we limited them to long shots which, given their strike force, was some achievement. We defended brilliantly, with every one of us putting our bodies in the way as they prepared to shoot. Physically and mentally, we seemed to be playing on a different level to anything I had seen before. At the final whistle, having held them to a goalless draw on their own ground and in all that adversity, with the spirit and the character that we had shown, we really started to feel that we had gained a psychological blow over Forest. It was great to go over and celebrate what felt like a moral victory with our fans. Later, in the lead up to the second game, I read comments in the press that the Forest players were annoyed by our attitude. They claimed we were behaving as if we had won the tie and that it was all over. We certainly knew it was not all over and that we would have a huge test at the Liberty Stadium. We simply shared with our fans the excitement of what we had achieved.

For the second leg, our stadium was rocking from

the time we warmed up and to the final whistle. It was the best atmosphere I've ever experienced at the Liberty Stadium. Many of the commentators said at the end of the match that it was one of those games to make the hairs on the back of your neck stand up. It was obvious from the start that their manager, Billy Davies, had decided to go for all-out attack. It was very close at the start of the game, with chances for both teams. Then Leon Britton, who doesn't shoot all that often, put us ahead with a great shot into the top corner. It was exactly what we needed, and that was shortly followed by Stephen Dobbie scoring a wonderful individual goal after nutmegging Luke Chambers and calmly slotting the ball past Forest keeper, Lee Camp. It was 2–0 going into half-time, and we were confident but wary of a very attack-minded Forest side.

I suppose it was always going to happen that an ex-Cardiff City striker would put them back in the game, and that's exactly what happened. When Rob Earnshaw scored to make it 2–1, it set up a nerve-racking final 20 minutes. I think that last period of the game was probably the most exciting football you will ever see at any level. They were playing with what seemed like two at the back and eight up front. I remember turning to Ashley Williams and saying, 'Ash, where are all these red shirts coming from?' Being a defender and captain at this point, along with Ash and Tatey, we were just trying to organize and focus the players around us, as well as concentrating on our own jobs whilst under intense pressure. Not easy when you can hardly hear yourself think with the noise of the crowd so loud! You felt the tension of the crowd. But our defence held it all together and right at the death Forest won a corner kick. Even their goalkeeper had come up to try and help them score the equalising goal, as they were desperate to take the game into extra time. We managed to scramble the ball clear and when Darren Pratley latched on to the loose ball he dribbled it to the halfway line. I shouted at him to take it to the corner. But, instead, he attempted an audacious shot into the empty net. It was an awfully long way, and when the ball finally hit the back of the net, it blew the roof off! The crowd went absolutely mental, as did the players. There was less than a minute left and I could see the manager doing his now famous run along the touchline. He was moving so fast that Mark Gower couldn't catch him. I ran into the Forest half, and went crazy on my own for as long as I could.

My family asked me afterwards, 'What were you doing all on your own in their half after Prats had scored?' It is something I often do in a match when we have just scored. I had been so focused on the game that I didn't realize that there was barely a minute left. Prats had run back into our half of the pitch, and all our players had followed him. It meant that Forest could take the restart, even though we weren't in position. The thinking behind my camping in the opponents' half is that it stops the opposition from kicking off. It's a decision I now half regret, because it looked like a decent pile on, on top of Prats! The full-time whistle went and it was just an unbelievable feeling. The team went upstairs and out into the stand. There were thousands of our fans on the pitch. The whole place was rocking and buzzing, with the ecstatic fans chanting and singing songs. The atmosphere was unbelievable and no one who was lucky enough to be there that night will ever forget it. All the players went out on the town and enjoyed a fabulous celebration.

A couple of days later, after all the wild joy and excitement, what had happened began to sink in. We were on our way to Wembley to attempt to become the first ever Welsh side to reach the Premiership. With that realization, it seemed to me that my excitement was mixed with other emotions, such as pressure, anxiety and nervousness. Plus the added worry whether I would be able to get tickets for all those who wanted them. It was amazing how, after the victory over Forest, loads of people who I hadn't seen or spoken to for years telephoned or texted me to remind me that I was their friend and could I get them tickets!

One of the problems we faced was that very few at the club were equipped to deal with what was happening. In the build-up to the final there were 20 or 30 camera crews from all over the world wanting a slice of everything we players were doing. On top of that, there were 40 or more journalists wanting interviews; they'd get hold of a mobile number and leaving countless texts and voice messages. The Wembley game is billed as the richest one-off game in sport, with a prize of £90 million and Premier League football which is regularly broadcast to all corners of the world. The pressure was immense and sometimes draining.

Whilst it was great to have such recognition for

what we had achieved at Swansea, it was also in danger of disrupting our preparation for the big game. This is where Brendan Rodgers dealt with everything superbly as a manager should do. He had been to big finals with Chelsea. He drew up a schedule which we all followed. There were days allocated specifically for the press, and he also sorted out ticket allocation for the team and many other aspects. His planning was so important, as it left four clear days for us to concentrate on nothing but the game.

On the Saturday before the final we trained at Arsenal's training ground. As we did our final preparations for the game, the gaffer was brilliant at keeping everything light and jovial. It was amazing how he managed to create such a relaxed atmosphere, but with undertones also of preparing for war. The facilities were magnificent and we joked with the gaffer that if we got to the Premiership, we would demand the same, including the hydro pools. Somehow we couldn't imagine the Gunners' stars being happy to share our training base and shower and changing rooms along with members of the public at the Virgin Active Health & Racquets Club, off Junction 43 on the M4!

On the Sunday afternoon a tour of Wembley was arranged for us. On the Saturday night the stadium had hosted the European Cup final between Manchester United and Barcelona. I was impressed to see how quickly they were rearranging all the advertising from UEFA Champions League to the Championship Npower signs. We were taken into the dressing rooms so that we wouldn't feel that we were in an unfamiliar place the next day. I was hoping that Lionel Messi or Xavi had left their washbags or football boots in the lockers. Unsurprisingly I was to find nothing! Getting our bearings was so important. We went out on to the pitch and stood there for about 20 minutes, staring up at this massive bowl-shaped stadium and at that point, I believed that it was definitely the best stadium I'd ever been about to play in, and I think that went for most of us. It was so impressive. I'd visited the old Wembley, but the new one was something else, and the fact that I would be playing there in 24 hours' time was even better. The gaffer pointed out where our families would be and I looked around and imagined it heaving with Swansea and Reading fans and visualised them there. I realized how clever the gaffer had been in exposing us to all this before the actual match. He had done everything possible to relax the players and not distract us, so there was no room left in our heads to worry about anything except playing this game.

We returned to the hotel and the management kept everything as normal as possible. We stayed in the same hotel as Blackpool had done the previous year before they went on to beat Cardiff City – so were all hoping this was a lucky omen.

The whole team was bubbling and it was that anticipation that gave me a bad night's sleep on the eve of the big game. I was so happy to appreciate that only a year on from just missing out on the play-offs under Paulo, I would now be leading the team out at Wembley. Despite the excitement, I wasn't feeling great. Between the semi-final legs and the final, I had had two cortisone injections to try and relieve my back pain and also pain-killing injections every day to help get me through training. I had also lost a fair amount of weight because of a virus I had picked up the previous week. When I look at the pictures of me from that game, I looked so pale and gaunt. Normally I weigh around the 85 kg mark for games, but for the final I was 79 kg. I couldn't have been in any worse condition on the eve of such an important match. I fought against all the negative feelings. I was the captain and I had to lead by example. Besides, you'd have had to kill me to stop me from playing in that final.

We left the hotel late morning and the bus drive to Wembley seemed to take forever. When we approached Wembley, a sea of black and white came into view – the Jack Army was out in force! As the bus prepared to go into the underground tunnel that led to the drop-off point, all of the boys looked around at all these faces from Swansea, with their flags, banners, horns, wigs, face paint, costumes etc. I thought to myself we can't let these fans down, nor our family and friends, who were also there in numbers.

During a discussion between players and management in the week leading up to the game, the gaffer put forward the idea that it was important to do everything together on the big day. It was agreed that we should not walk on to the pitch separately before the game, nor should we spread out. We took this advice and when we arrived at Wembley we got off the coach and walked together on to the turf in our suits. Being captain, the gaffer wanted me to lead these things. I believe this togetherness helped us greatly. The manager didn't really have to say too much to us in the dressing room about the game, as we were all ready and focused. As we all went out together again for the warm-up, it was amazing to see all those Swansea fans in the stadium. After watching the game on DVD, I realized what a great job Kevin Johns, our match day announcer, did in pumping up the Jack Army for action. At the time the other players and myself were not really aware of what was going on as we were so focused on the match in hand.

Leading the team out at Wembley was one of the proudest moments of my life. The noise from the 40,000-plus Swans fans was deafening, and the Reading fans made a fair din too. The 86,581 at the stadium was a record for a Championship play-off final. After all the introductions, handshakes and toss of the coin, it was time for business. Before kick-off, I got all the players into a huddle and said to them, 'We've worked to get to this point, not just in this season but our entire careers. We'll come off this pitch at the end with no regrets.' I mentioned several reasons why we were doing this, but as a group and with what we had all been through, the most important reason in my mind was to do it for Besian Idrizaj, who had died in his sleep the summer before the season started in Austria. The striker was only 22. I knew his family would be watching and he'd been such a motivation for us that season. At the end of the huddle, as always, I said 'Whatever happens in the game we must keep going to the very end no matter what.'

As the game started, the Royals were slightly on top for the first 20 minutes. Although their main threat was supposed to be Shane Long, who had caused havoc for Cardiff City in the other semi-final, as a defence we managed to snuff him out. The main danger was their winger Jimmy Kébé, who had just returned from injury. He was very quick and direct and they were trying to get the ball to him as much as possible, but after the initial threat I thought that Tatey marked him out of the game superbly. Then, after 20 minutes the whole complexion of the game changed. Nathan Dyer made a clever move into their box and was about to shoot when he was brought down. Royals defender, Khizanishvili, was already on a yellow card, and the foul on Nathan warranted at least another yellow which meant the defender should have been sent off. I didn't think about it at the time – I was just happy we had a penalty. Scott Sinclair was an excellent penalty taker and had been all season, so I was confident of a score. He converted the penalty perfectly. We were on our way. A minute or so later Stephen Dobbie showed his pace down our right flank, something which he's not renowned for, easing past Ian Harte on to the loose ball, then he sent over a perfect cross for Scotty Sinclair to slot home and make it 2–0. I remember thinking, God it's not supposed to be this easy! Just as we were thinking it couldn't get any better, it did! Again we broke down our right-hand side and, after a half clearance by a Reading defender, Dobbie was in the perfect position to crash home a beautiful volley from 20 yards. I was directly behind the shot and, like Dobbie, I knew it was in from the moment it left his foot. I just couldn't believe the scoreline, 3–0 going into the half-time break. That was the stuff of dreams.

Once in the changing room, it has to be said that none of us was getting over-excited. It was calm, and the gaffer made observations about how we could improve in the second half. Although we had got ourselves into a fantastic position, we never do anything easily at Swansea City. We knew Reading had nothing to lose and would come out hard in the second half. We had to try and refocus and match them for the fight. I still believe that, had we not been three goals to the good, Reading would never have come out as gung ho as they did. As the second half proceeded, it became obvious that we had lost some of our concentration and had stopped doing a lot of what we were good at. They were now pinning us back in our half and it seemed at times that they had extra men on the pitch. Within five minutes of the restart, they pulled a goal back from a corner – an unlucky Joe Allen unknowingly deflecting the ball into our own net. One of the things mentioned in the dressing room just before we came back out for the second half was for us to make a solid start and give nothing away, especially for the first 20 minutes. But, we did the exact opposite, and only six minutes after conceding the first goal, they scored again from another corner. It was my man, and I was inches away from getting my head on the ball. It is one of the worst feelings as a defender when the man you're supposed to be marking scores a goal. To be fair, it was a great header by Matthew Mills, but that didn't help our cause. It meant that now we were only one goal ahead, and there was plenty of time for Reading to equalize and even to go on to win the game. The Royals now had the momentum and, as much as you try to remain calm as players and not panic, we were in grave danger of being on the wrong end of one of the best comebacks of all time.

It was definitely becoming twitchy-bum time for our fans. On the hour mark Reading broke again. Ashley Williams did a great sliding block from a Jem Karacan shot, the block deflected the ball on to our post, it rebounded off the post and fell straight to their striker, Noel Hunt, only ten yards out. He had the whole open goal at his mercy and, 99 times out of 100, that scenario would have ended as a goal. You have a split-second as a defender to try to get some sort of block or touch to try to stop the shot. Mercifully, I managed to get my outstretched right boot to the flight of the ball and deflect it away.

Since the game many people have come up to me and asked about that block. Some newspapers and pundits were calling it the £90 million block, but it was just a defender's instinct to try to get some part of my body in the way. At the time I didn't really notice, but I think that was the turning point in the game for us. If that had gone in, then who knows what would have happened, but my guess is that it wouldn't have been nice. If we'd lost the game from the position we were in at half-time, I don't think I would have been able to show my face in Swansea ever again. I would have moved to the moon. Instead we refocused. We started playing our football again and doing what we do best, passing and moving the ball around. We took back control of the game. We were starting to create good chances ourselves, and were an attacking force once again. The gaffer brought on Darren Pratley to stiffen up the midfield and to be a bit more of a physical presence. It was a good substitution as Prats broke up a lot of Reading's play. With ten minutes to go, Tatey intercepted a Royals pass, strode forward with the ball, before feeding the ball to Fabio Borini inside their box. Thankfully their fullback, Andy Griffin, made a rash challenge and brought Fabio down. Phil Dowd pointed straight to the spot and we were awarded our second penalty of the game.

I didn't know what to do. Should I watch or look away and wait for the crowd to let me know whether we had scored? In the end I watched it on the screen behind the goal where Scott Sinclair coolly tucked away his second penalty of the afternoon and gave him his hat-trick. We knew that we still had ten minutes to hang on to the lead, but that fourth goal was the cushion we needed. You could also see that the Reading players were physically drained. That fourth goal had knocked the fight out of them.

I was a relieved man, because five minutes before the penalty, my right foot was starting to feel numb and I remember thinking, I hope this doesn't go into extra time. I'm not sure I'll last. I was struggling. I think it was my body just shutting down after what I had put it through over the last three to four weeks, all those injections plus the virus. But we saw the game out and when Phil Dowd blew the final whistle, it was the greatest feeling of relief I've ever experienced. I celebrated with the players who were nearest to me, Darren Pratley, Tatey, Mark Gower and Dorus and then the others came and joined us. I, along with some of the other players, had been on the other side of this emotion when we lost the play-off final to Barnsley. At the moment of celebration,

I realized that my life would change forever. I was now a Premiership footballer with Swansea City. If it hadn't been for that result, I probably wouldn't be writing this book. The week leading up to that final, I had Besian on my mind. If we won, I wanted to do something to show his family and friends that, at our greatest moment, we had not forgotten him. So, I had 40 T-shirts made, inscribed in memory of him. I had given them to our kit lady, Suzanne Eames, and asked her to hand them out if we won. So we donned the T-shirts in preparation for our celebrations.

I was then asked by an official to lead the players up the steps to collect the Cup. As a kid I had seen many famous players do this at Wembley, the home of football. A couple of nights earlier, Lionel Messi, one of the greatest players in the world, had done it with his star-studded Barcelona. Now it was my turn. It was just unbelievable. I wanted to savour every moment, every second. I had told Tatey that I was going to count every one of the 107 steps on my way to fetch the Cup. By the time I'd done 20 steps I thought, OK now where's the stair lift? I'm knackered! As we got to the top of the steps, they told us to wait before making the final few steps up to where our fans and Cup were waiting. We were jumping manically, shouting and chanting, 'We are Premier League.' I had time to reflect again and thought 'in a few seconds I'm going to be holding that Cup aloft.' As I made it up onto the balcony, looking out on all of the 40,000 plus Swans fans was truly a special moment, something I will never forget. Amazing, spine-tingling. They started handing the medals to the first few of us, and the sponsor then passed the

Cup to me. I kissed it and lifted it up above my head to the huge roars of the Jack Army. That moment was so special, and along with my engagement to Lexy and the birth of our daughter Remy, it was up there as one of the proudest moments of my life. Tatey was standing next to me and I passed him the Cup. Looking back at him I should have milked the Cup, raising it a little bit more, hung on to it for longer. I began to think that we should have stayed here doing this for at least another hour! As I moved along, I caught sight of the chairman and the board members, the people who work in the offices, and I realized that their lives would also be changed forever. It was great to give them this moment too, as they had also worked so hard for our club for a number of years, and it was great to see them enjoying this.

Down on the pitch, it was time to party and get sprayed with champagne and see all the fans close up. I looked for my family and friends. Then I came across a person dressed as an orange and green daffodil. The silly-looking daffodil was crying and, as I looked a little closer, I realized that it was my brother! He had been out all weekend on his stag do and all his mates had made him dress up like this for the game. It was hilarious. I could see Lexy and Remy, my mum and dad, my whole family and friends. I was so proud that they were all there. You never want that lap of honour to end. All those songs, everyone dancing, it was just perfect. Back in the changing rooms, the partying continued with wild celebrations. Many of us didn't even bother getting showered or changed before going to see our families and friends; we just headed upstairs in our kit, still soaked from a mixture of sweat and champagne. Eventually, after doing all the media interviews and getting back into our club suits, we got on to the team coach and headed back to continue the party in Swansea. However, I felt really drained. Even though the bus journey home was an extremely happy place to be, I didn't react in the way I thought I would. I wasn't going crazy and I didn't want to get so drunk that I wouldn't be able to savour the moment. And by now my foot had gone totally numb and was really painful. But the journey back was surreal. A sea of black and white made its way back down the M4 and piled into every service station on the way cheering and singing. One great memory was pulling up at the tollbooth on the Severn Bridge. The queue of cars, vans and buses stretched way back, but it was like a carnival, people hanging out of the windows, waving flags, beeping horns – some even out dancing on the motorway.

My roommate, Mark Gower, had no such worries. He downed a small bottle of vodka on the bus and got absolutely wrecked. When the bus pulled up in Swansea outside Morgan's hotel, Mark stepped off the bus and went to head one of the balloons tied to the railings. He missed, hit his head on one of the railings, gashed the top of his head wide open, and his night was over before it had even began. He was patched up and taken to one of the rooms in the hotel where he was put to bed and left to sleep it off.

It was so good to sit with my family at the party. My father was overjoyed and my mother was very tipsy, crying with joy. I sat with Lexy, just enjoying the whole atmosphere. I was so happy. My brother was still on his weekend-long stag party; he and his mates had all come back as well. Everyone partied into the early hours. It was a running joke at my brother's wedding that his own mother turned up at his stag do, and actually ended up more drunk than the stag!

The next day, it was arranged for us to parade in an open-top bus around the city centre. I felt much better than I had done the night before. The game had drained me, but now I was ready to really party and enjoy a good drink. Unfortunately, the other boys were seriously hungover, and didn't want to entertain the thought of another drink.

I suppose, as a player, when you are told that you are going to parade through the streets, the greatest fear is that no one will turn up. But, on this occasion, that was an impossibility. We had done the same thing with Roberto when we won League One, but the turnout this day totally outstripped the previous one. There were thousands more people this time – what seemed like the whole of Swansea were in attendance! Everywhere there were flags, scarves, mums and dads and thousands of smiling children's faces. It was good for the lads to see how much this promotion meant to the city. I sat with Tatey at the front of the bus and just soaked up the whole amazing experience.

Before the game I thought that if we won, the celebrations would go on forever, but they didn't. After the parade, everyone went their separate ways. We were already well into what would have been our summer break, and we would meet up again soon for pre-season. On 1 June Rod Stewart sang to a packed Liberty Stadium. He invited the Swans' players to join him on stage, but with most of the boys now away, only six of us plus most of the management showed up. I think that standing backstage waiting to meet Rod was more unnerving than being at Wembley, as walking out onto the stage was another surreal moment. There we were, on stage with Rod Stewart, in front of a packed Liberty Stadium. He was moving down the line, shaking everyone's hand. As he got closer, I just thought I'm going in for the hug! When he got to me I just hugged him and he said, 'How's your mum?' I must remember to ask her how he knows her!

Chapter Nine

THE 2011–12 SEASON will never be forgotten by Swansea City fans. We became the first Welsh team to make it into the Premiership and it was the first time that the Swans had played at the highest level of league football for nearly 30 years. As we approached the new season it was also a memorable time for the players, as only a few of us had played in the Premiership before and none of us with any real regularity. Despite my appearances for the Saints, I think all of us felt that this was a real journey into the unknown. Many of us would have watched the big teams with their star players on *Match of the Day* and Sky Sports over the years. I had to pinch myself when I realized that for the next ten months I would be playing against them.

Back in July 2011, we looked at the fixture list and realized that we were heading for a baptism of fire. It couldn't have been more difficult than Manchester City, Arsenal and Chelsea for your first three away games.

As in every season there are always comings and goings of players. We welcomed Danny Graham, Steven Caulker, Michel Vorm, then a little later Wayne Routledge and Leroy Lita into the squad. I had a difficult summer with my fitness. My foot had not really recovered in time for pre-season training with the squad. It was the first time in my career that I had missed the pre-season. What was to be the most important and exciting season the club had ever known might have turned into a nightmare for me. I was desperate to get the feeling back in my foot. Our fitness coach, Ryland Morgans, and physios, Kate Rees and Richard Buchanan, worked with me all through pre-season but, unfortunately, I was unable to make it for the opening match away to Manchester City. I was gutted not to be leading the boys out for the Swans' first ever Premiership match.

I travelled with the squad and, as the team captain, even if not playing, I would I have had a role to play. I have always been a voice in the dressing room and I use it to have a quiet word in the ear of some of the players or gee others up. Our squad is not overly loud, so they are all used to hearing my voice. As a senior player I think it's important that I play my part in helping and encouraging the players.

Walking down the tunnel before the pre-match warm up, I looked at all these star-studded players such as David Silva, Mario Balotelli, Yaya Touré, Sergio Agüero to name but a few. I said to a few of the boys, 'We know all their names, but I bet they don't know any of ours.' Just before kick-off, Alan Tate, Leon Britton and I were chatting and saying that, just a few years earlier, a point from an away trip to Yeovil would have been regarded as a great result. Now, in five minutes time, we would be doing battle against one of the richest teams in the world, full of household names, in a Premier League fixture, the best league in the world – mind-blowing really. As soon as the final whistle went after our play-off final win back in May, the so-called pundits and experts had us as favourites to be relegated straight back to the Championship. A hard thing to accept, with not even a ball being kicked. But we as players and management knew that we were there on merit and were determined to show that.

We played well for a hour and were holding our own. Then a certain Mr Agüero came off the bench to make his debut and produced a devastating display. He scored two and set up another as we went on to lose 4–0, a scoreline which was very harsh on us. Despite the loss, we could hold our heads high and take many positives from the game. We played well and with Nathan and Scott on the wings and Danny up the middle, we stretched them without punishing them. It marked the arrival of Michel Vorm, who produced a man of the match display with some outstanding saves, world class in fact.

Before the start of the season we were confident that we would survive in the Premiership, and not only survive but compete well with everyone. It's one thing to think that, but you need proof. At the end of that game, as we chatted in the dressing room, I think the feeling was that we had given a good account of ourselves, despite the scoreline.

Just as we had been amazed when we looked at the fixture list and saw our first three away games, we found it equally unbelievable when we saw who our opponents would be for the first ever Premiership match at our Liberty Stadium. If someone was writing our season as a film script, then this is probably what they would have written too. The visitors would be Wigan Athletic, managed by none other than Roberto Martinez. As the players talked about the game, we were all keen to win for the fans and to get one over on Roberto. As it turned out, the goalless draw was probably a fair result. We dominated the game for the first 60 or 70 minutes but couldn't quite convert our chances. Then, they came back at us strongly. Wigan hit the post and Michel made a couple of great saves, including a penalty. Michel was already proving what a great goalkeeper he was and the perfect replacement for Dorus de Vries who had decided to leave us.

I was very surprised when Dorus left in the summer and signed for Wolverhampton Wanderers. I think it was a poor football decision from Dorus who would have been the number one goalkeeper had he stayed at the Liberty and also given him the Premiership football that he craved for. I am sure that financial considerations played a big part in his decision as I believe he was guaranteed a financial package for three years, even if Wolves were relegated, an assurance that the Swans could not have given him. Dorus had been an integral part of the team and was a big influence on the pitch, as well as being a good keeper. Many of our attacks started with Dorus, and he had great distribution skills. As well as playing out short to his defenders, he could pick out players 40 to 50 yards from his goal. I couldn't imagine Mick McCarthy allowing him to play in this way, as that's not how Wolves play. Anyway, it was Dorus's decision and I have nothing but the greatest respect for him, both as a goalkeeper and a friend.

It was a big worry that, when Dorus left the club, finding a replacement would be quite a task. The goalkeeper is an important position in any team, but even more so for us as it's where we start all our attacks from – our style of play is based around playing from the goalkeeper. Much like Dorus, the replacement had to be a footballer as well as a goalkeeper, which was not an easy requirement to find. I thought Dorus would be a hard act to follow, but Michel has been fantastic and proved to be not just as good as Dorus, but probably even better. Michel has to go down as one of the gaffer's best signings when he signed him from Utrecht for a bargain £1.5 million in the close season.

Following the Manchester City and Wigan games, we then went another two games without scoring. We lost 0–1 away to Arsenal and drew 0–0 at home to Sunderland. The media made a huge deal about the fact that the new boys of Swansea had failed to find the back of the net in 360 minutes of football. As a team we began to realize that the pressure the media puts you under is a lot more intense than when you are in the Championship or Leagues One and Two. When you are playing at that level, the media become interested in you once a week, just before your next game. Once you're in the Premiership, the coverage is 24 hours a day, seven days a week. Suddenly, every aspect of your game and form is being analysed. We realized that the pressure about the lack of goals was coming from outside the club. We were not feeling it amongst the team. We were confident in the way we were playing and believed that the goals would come. It would have been different if we had not been creating chances, but we were. Danny Graham had gone close on so many occasions and it was obvious that he was not stressed by the situation.

Our fifth Premiership game silenced our critics with a 3–0 win over West Bromwich Albion at the Liberty Stadium. There were a couple of firsts that day, as Scott Sinclair became the first player to score a Premiership goal outside England. I also made my first Premiership appearance for Swansea. It felt amazing. I, like Tatey and Leon, had now played in every division for Swansea City. But what made it even more special was that I had now become the only player in the history of the club to have captained the team in every division as well. To top this special day off, it was our first ever Premiership win too. Perfect, all of this will stay with me forever.

In October we looked on course to gain our first away win at Molyneux. Of course, the longer you go with out a win, the more the media attention intensifies and the more it becomes a monkey on your back. We went in at half-time a worthy 2–0 ahead, after goals from Danny Graham and Joe Allen. With eight minutes to go we were still 2–0 up and were coasting to the three points. Then, Wolves scored twice in two minutes, and they snatched a point. In the dressing room afterwards, we were all bitterly disappointed. It felt as though we had been beaten rather than having just gained our first away point in the Premiership. Games like that often do feel like a defeat, but in many ways it was a turning point for us and our season. We realized that we could compete away from home at this level.

That confidence was strengthened when we played at Anfield on 5 November. Before the season had started, this was a game that many of us had looked forward to. Liverpool away at Anfield was a visit that was so full of history for anyone who likes or is involved in football. At that point in the season I would say that that was the biggest game so far for us. During the warm-up I shared a joke with Ashley Williams. I said to him that the strikers we faced today, Andy Carroll and Luis Suarez, cost Liverpool a combined total of £58 million in transfer fees, whilst Ash and I cost Swansea a combined £400,000. You can easily come up with stats like that for every game that we play in this league. But that's what makes it so exciting for us. Playing against these sorts of players are fantastic experiences. We played excellently that day, and at what many would consider the birthplace of passing football we gave them a bit of a lesson. We controlled large periods of the game, our passing was crisp and some of the movement and play we showed was fantastic.

Although Andy Carroll hit the crossbar early on and Michel Vorm made a great save from Luis Suarez, we had our chances as well. None better, in fact, than when the ball fell kindly to Mark Gower inside their box in front of a packed Kop, right at the death. I think half of us were already on our way to celebrate, with Mark expecting the ball to hit the back of the net. Imagine that! All of us celebrating what would have probably been the winning goal in front of the legendary Kop end of Anfield. Unfortunately, he blazed the ball over the bar. At the final whistle, after earning a well deserved draw, we went over to where all the travelling Swans fans were, and joined them in celebrating what was a mammoth effort from both players and fans alike. But, what put the icing on our performance was the fact that, when we headed for the tunnel, we were clapped off by the Liverpool fans who had stayed behind to show their appreciation of our performance. That was a touch of class from a knowledgeable crowd. It was great for us to assess ourselves against a team packed with top players at Premiership level and at a club with such a great tradition.

Our next game was at home to Manchester United. This was probably the game our fans had been looking forward to more than any other. United were the first top four team to come to the Liberty Stadium. It was a sellout game and for days before the match there was a huge buzz around the city. We had played a couple of Premiership teams over the years at our Liberty, but none of the calibre of Manchester United. They are the biggest British club, with a star-studded side who have been champions a record 19 times. Because of all the hype about the game, I was worried that maybe the occasion would get to the team. I tried to lighten the tension in the player huddle before kick-off. I went through the usual motivational stuff, then ended my talk with 'Bagsey Rooney's shirt.' It didn't have the desired effect. We didn't play very well in the first half. We gave them far too much respect. At half-time the gaffer had a real go at us, and told us we were too much in awe of them. He told us to go out in the second half and show them what we could do. Our second half performance was much better and, although we lost 0–1, I think we deserved a draw. The way we played in the second half against one of the top teams in Europe gave us great confidence. As we chatted after the game, we all agreed that we didn't want to be gallant losers. It was another important moment in our season and we seemed to be making good progress in each match.

Having played so well against Liverpool and Manchester United, the feeling was that it was important to beat one of these top sides. That happened in a fantastic match at the Liberty Stadium against Arsenal, which we won 3–2. It was billed as the battle of the passers. Both teams' philosophy is built upon retaining possession and the quick pass and move style. We outplayed a passing team at their own game. That result, in particular, put us on the football map. It was beamed out around the world on live TV. It gave us national and international recognition. Our players were now being talked about. Young players such as Joe Allen and Nathan Dyer were making massive progress, and Leon Britton was statistically one of the top passers in Europe. A fantastic achievement. I have to say that, in all my time at Swansea, Leon is the best player I have played with. He has played all across the midfield and even filled in at full-back occasionally. But he has made the holding midfield role an art. I believe he is one of the best in the Premiership in that position. He always makes himself available to receive the ball and never gives the ball away. His work rate is phenomenal. He is one of the best to have ever put on the white Swansea shirt.

Again it's the perception of many football commentators that British players can't play. We are showing them that our British players can, and squad mentality is something that Brendan Rodgers preaches all the time. Obviously, players who don't play don't like it, but we have great respect for each other and the gaffer. We have a unique squad in that way. We have players who are hungry for success. We all have a point to prove in one way or another, and we have such a close bond with each other that any new arrivals have to buy into our unique squad.

Whilst putting the finishing touches to this book, we're now in 12th position in the league on 43 points, which has secured our Premier League safety with three games still to play, and we're pushing for a top half finish. We have surprised many managers, teams and commentators with our football. Our aim from the start was to retain our Premiership status. We want to be here for a number of years.

In the time I have been at the club, we have achieved truly remarkable feats. We have come from the bottom division to the Premiership, the biggest, best and most exciting league in the world, and this in just seven seasons. The journey is far from over. This is where the hard work really begins. We have to try to build a club that can compete at all times. Our infrastructure, such as our training facilities, must be addressed and brought up to the level of the team. We must push forward for a private, fully-functioning facility and improve it year on year. We have no excuses now not to do that. We have built up an identity as a club which is now known not only in Britain but around the world. We have to use this to our advantage. If we can set up an academy and install good facilities, we can also expand our scouting network to attract young talent to the club and have all ages playing the Swansea way. It could pave the way for many more to make it to the first-team level, such as happened with Joe Allen and Jazz Richards. It would make Swansea an even more attractive club to play for and support.